PreK–K

Hooray for ART!

A Year's Worth of Arts-and-Crafts Projects

Your youngsters will love
creating arts-and-crafts projects
for these seasons:

Fall
Winter
Spring
Summer
Anytime

Managing Editor: Allison E. Ward

Editorial Team: Becky S. Andrews, Kimberley Bruck, Karen P. Shelton,
Diane Badden, Kimberly Brugger-Murphy, Cindy Daoust,
Leanne Stratton, Karen A. Brudnak, Sarah Hamblet,
Hope Rodgers, Dorothy C. McKinney

Production Team: Lisa K. Pitts, Pam Crane, Rebecca Saunders,
Jennifer Tipton Cappoen, Chris Curry, Theresa Lewis Goode, Clint Moore,
Greg D. Rieves, Barry Slate, Donna K. Teal, Zane Williard, Tazmen Carlisle,
Amy Kirtley-Hill, Kristy Parton, Cathy Edwards Simrell,
Lynette Dickerson, Mark Rainey

www.themailbox.com

Manufactured in the United States
10 9 8 7 6 5 4 3 2

P9-AGS-420

Table of Contents

Fall

We're Happy to Be Here!

Big smiles all around! That's what you'll see on little ones' faces as they make this simple project.

Supplies:

several small paper cups
shallow dishes of tempera
  paints in skin tones

9" x 12" construction paper
colored hole reinforcers
crayons

Steps:

1. Dip an upside-down cup in one color of paint.
2. Press the cup onto the construction paper repeatedly to make several circles.
3. Repeat Steps 1 and 2 with each remaining color of paint, overlapping circles. Set the project aside to dry.
4. Attach pairs of hole reinforcers to create eyes on several circles.
5. Use a crayon to add a smile to each circle with eyes.

Jill Davis—Grs. K–1 Multiage, Kendall-Whittier Elementary School, Tulsa, OK

Silly Reflections

Each child can start the day with a smile as he checks his image in his own cubby mirror.

Supplies:

6" x 9" craft foam
4" x 6" silver metallic wrapping paper
glue

markers
washable paint pens
adhesive Velcro fastener

Steps:

1. Glue the wrapping paper to the foam.
2. Use a marker to write your name at the bottom of the foam.
3. Use paint pens to decorate the foam frame.
4. Use Velcro fastener to attach the mirror to the back wall of the cubby.

Cindy S. Barber—Art, Saints Cecilia and James Catholic School, Thiensville, WI

Allyson Janet

Blue-Ribbon Writing

These prize-winning name ribbons emphasize letter-writing skills.

Supplies:

variety of 3" craft foam shapes
permanent marker

1½"-wide blue ribbon
glue

Steps:

1. Choose one foam shape for each letter in your name.
2. Write one letter from your name on each shape.
3. Place the ribbon vertically on a flat surface.
4. Glue each shape in order on the ribbon. Let it dry.
5. Cut the ribbon to size and then make a loop at the top and glue it in place to make a hanger.

Cindy S. Barber—Art, Saints Cecilia and James Catholic School, Thiensville, WI

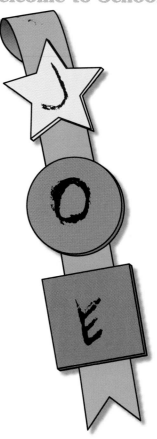

Shimmering Type

Hone keyboarding skills with this nifty name hanger. Display youngsters' creations around a computer keyboard cutout on a board titled "All Keyed Up About Our Names!"

Supplies:

access to a computer and printer
printer paper
scissors
Elmer's Shimmer 'N Shine washable art glaze

paintbrush
4" x 6" craft foam
glue
12" length of ribbon
clear packaging tape

Setup:

Help a child type her name on the computer. Enlarge the font and print the name. Trim around the printed name to create a card that is approximately 3" x 5".

Steps:

1. Lay the name card on a flat surface.
2. Brush on Shimmer 'N Shine glaze to cover the name. Let it dry.
3. Glue the name card to the foam. Let it dry.
4. Tape the ribbon to the foam to make a hanger.

Cindy S. Barber—Art

Timid Turtle

This warmhearted poem and turtle buddy will calm beginning-of-school jitters.

Supplies:

dark green construction paper turtle
light green oval to fit turtle (shell)
glue
4 dark green construction paper hearts
white paper heart with poem

light green construction paper
  heart slightly larger than the
  white paper heart (pocket)
red craft foam heart
glue

Steps:

1. Glue the shell on the turtle.
2. Glue the four green hearts on the shell.
3. Spread glue around the sides and bottom of the pocket, leaving an opening at the top; then glue the pocket on the underside of the turtle.
4. Glue the poem on the pocket. Let the turtle dry.
5. Read the poem and put the foam heart inside the pocket.

Sue Fleischmann—Preschool, Child and Family Centers of Excellence, Waukesha, WI

The timid turtle said, "I don't want to go!"
Mama Turtle said, "School is important, you know."
So she gave the timid turtle a very special heart,
To remind him of her love whenever they're apart.

First-Day Photo Magnet

Here's a colorful craft that captures each child's first day of school and makes a picture-perfect parent gift! Watch for back-to-school sales to have extra crayons on hand for this worthwhile project.

Supplies:

3" x 5" craft foam
3" x 5" child's photograph
8 new crayons
paper towel
glue
adhesive magnetic tape

Steps:

1. Spread a thin layer of glue onto the back of the photograph, and place it on top of the foam. Place a paper towel on top of the photograph, and press down slightly.
2. Carefully apply two lines of glue along one outside edge of the photograph.
3. Place two crayons on the glue and hold them in place for a few minutes.
4. Repeat Steps 2 and 3 for the remaining three sides of the photograph.
5. When the glue is dry, attach two strips of magnetic tape to the back of the foam.

Sue Fleischmann—Preschool, Child and Family Centers of Excellence, Waukesha, WI

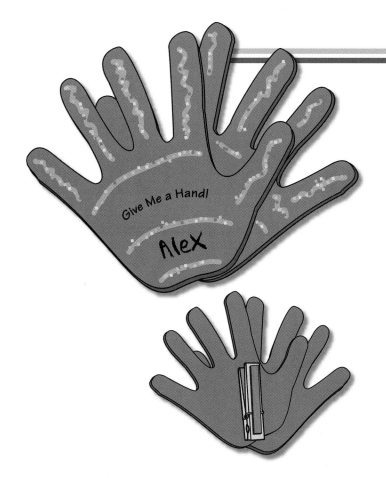

Give Me a Hand!

What a handy way to display student work at school or at home!

Supplies:

2 craft foam hands   permanent marker
glue   spring-type clothespin
glitter glue   adhesive magnetic tape

Steps:

1. Glue the hands together. *(Write "Give Me a Hand!" across the hands.)*
2. Write your name at the bottom of the hands.
3. Use glitter glue to add decorations.
4. Attach a strip of magnetic tape to the clothespin.
5. Glue the clothespin onto the back of the hands. Let the glue dry.

Fitting Frame

Use this adjustable frame to display all sorts of artwork throughout the school year.

Supplies:

two 2" x 12" yellow craft foam strips
two 1½" x 2" pink craft foam rectangles (erasers)
scissors
glue
markers
washable paint pens
adhesive magnetic tape

Steps:

1. Cut one end of each foam strip into a point to resemble a pencil.
2. Glue a pink eraser onto the uncut end of each pencil.
3. Write your name in large letters on each craft foam pencil.
4. Use markers or paint pens to decorate the pencils as desired.
5. Attach a strip of magnetic tape to the back of each pencil.
6. Use the pencils to hold artwork (top and bottom) on a metal surface.

Cindy S. Barber—Art, Saints Cecilia and James Catholic School, Thiensville, WI

Personal Placemat

Alphabet sponges add a personal touch to these useful placemats.

Supplies:

12" x 18" construction paper
alphabet sponges
tempera paints
markers

Steps:

1. Choose the alphabet sponges needed to spell your name.
2. Dip each sponge in paint and print each letter on the paper in order. Let the paint dry.
3. Use markers to draw a picture above your name.
   (Laminate the placemats.)

Paper-Chain Pals

Getting acquainted with classmates and artistic expression go hand in hand with this dandy display!

Supplies:
markers
multicultural paper doll
assorted craft supplies
glue
tape

Steps:

1. Draw a face on the paper doll.
2. Use craft supplies and glue to add hair and clothes to personalize the paper doll.
3. Write your name on the front of the doll.
4. Share your pal with the class. *(Tape the pals along a wall as shown.)*

Keely Peasner—Preschool, Midlands Kiddie Korral and Head Start, Tacoma, WA

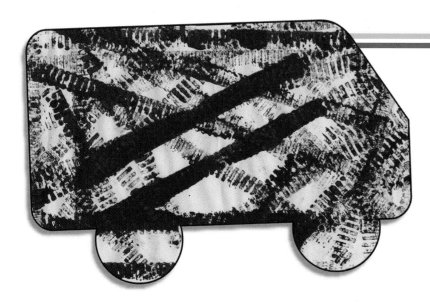

Makin' Tracks

Beep! Beep! The wheels on this busy bus drive youngsters along artistic tracks!

Supplies:
12" x 18" yellow construction paper
black tempera paint
toy bus
scissors

Steps:

1. Place the yellow paper on a flat surface.
2. Roll the bus through the paint to coat the wheels.
3. Drive the bus across the yellow paper.
4. Repeat until the paper has several tracks. Let the paint dry.
5. Cut out a large school bus shape from the yellow paper.

Jill Davis—Grs. K–1 Multiage, Kendall-Whittier Elementary School, Tulsa, OK

Harvest Headband

"Ears" a corny craft students will enjoy making and wearing. Turn the ears up or down for two stylish variations!

Supplies:

2" x 18" brown construction
   paper strip (headband)
construction paper scraps
markers
two 8" yellow construction
   paper corncobs

2 green construction
   paper corn husks
glue
scissors
tape

Steps:

1. Use markers and paper scraps to decorate the headband.
2. Glue a husk to each corncob.
3. Glue each ear of corn to the headband. *(Size the headband and tape the ends of the strip together.)*

Keely Peasner—Preschool, Midlands Kiddie Korral and Head Start, Tacoma, WA

Showy Sunflower

Show off these textured sunflowers on a spectacular harvest display!

Supplies:

3" yellow construction paper circle
5" yellow construction paper circle
5" green construction paper half circle
small scraps of brown craft foam

scissors
glue

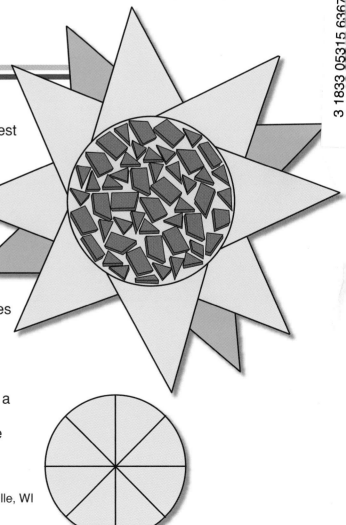

Setup:

Cut the five-inch yellow circle into eight equal-sized wedges as shown. Cut the half circle into four equal-sized wedges in the same manner.

Steps:

1. Glue the yellow wedges, points out, to the circle to form a flower.
2. Glue the green wedges behind the yellow wedges in the same manner to form leaves.
3. Glue the foam pieces on the circle.

Cindy S. Barber—Art, Saints Cecilia and James Catholic School, Thiensville, WI

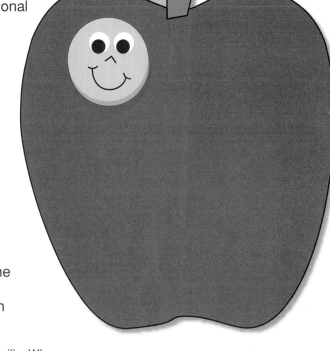

Worm's House

This thee-dimensional worm makes a cozy home of traditional apple art.

Supplies:

red construction paper apple
brown construction paper stem
green construction paper leaf
glue
1½" green craft foam circle (worm)
2 wiggle eyes stickers
fine black marker
double-sided adhesive foam dot

Steps:

1. Glue the stem and leaf to the apple.
2. Put the wiggle eyes stickers on the worm; then draw the remaining facial features.
3. Adhere the adhesive dot to the back of the worm. Then attach the dot to the apple.

Cindy S. Barber—Art, Saints Cecilia and James Catholic School, Thiensville, WI

Apple Collage

In red, green, or yellow, this collage creation looks almost good enough to eat!

Supplies:

red, green, or yellow
   magazine scraps
construction paper
dish of diluted white glue
paintbrush

scissors
green construction paper leaf
brown construction paper
   stem

Steps:

1. Tear the magazine scraps into small pieces.
2. Brush glue on the construction paper; then cover the paper with the magazine scraps. Let the glue dry.
3. Cut out an apple from the collage.
4. Glue the leaf and stem to the top of the apple.

Jill Davis—Grs. K–1 Multiage, Kendall-Whittier Elementary, Tulsa, OK

Apple Twist Prints

Try this twist on apple printing. Then make an "a-peel-ing" fall bulletin board by displaying a class set!

Supplies:

black construction paper
apple halves and quarters

red, yellow, and green
tempera paint
shallow dish

Setup:

Allow an hour or two for the apple sections to air-dry before painting. When it's time to paint, pour a dot of each color into a shallow dish. The colors should overlap one another.

Steps:

1. Dip the cut side of an apple into the paint dish and twist.
2. Carefully press the apple onto the construction paper; then lift it off.
3. Repeat the steps until the page has several prints.

Jill Davis—Grs. K–1 Multiage, Kendall-Whittier Elementary, Tulsa, OK

Inside-Out Pumpkin

After observing the inside of a real pumpkin, invite your youngsters to make this artistic version!

Supplies:

large orange construction paper pumpkin
smaller white construction paper pumpkin
shallow box (slightly larger than white
     pumpkin)
dish of orange tempera paint
marble
spoon
small brown construction paper rectangle (stem)
5 craft foam pumpkin seeds
glue

Steps:

1. Lay the white pumpkin in the box.
2. Dip the marble in the paint and put it in the box.
3. Tilt the box to roll the marble across the pumpkin several times.
4. Repeat Steps 2–3 until a desired effect is created. Set the pumpkin aside to dry.
5. Glue the painted pumpkin atop the orange pumpkin.
6. Glue the seeds and stem to the pumpkin.

Ada Goren, Winston-Salem, NC

Pudgy Pumpkin

This three-dimensional pumpkin makes a simple but colorful hanging decoration.

Supplies:

orange construction paper pumpkin
scissors
hole puncher
brown yarn
green construction paper
   scraps
glue
green curling ribbon

Steps:

1. Fold the pumpkin in half.
2. Beginning at the fold, cut slits in the pumpkin, as shown, stopping about one inch from the outer edge.
3. Unfold the pumpkin. *(Alternate pushing and pulling the strips to make the pumpkin pudgy.)*
4. Punch a hole in the top of the pumpkin.
5. Tie a loop of brown yarn through the hole.
6. Cut green scraps to look like leaves, and glue them near the yarn.
7. Thread green curling ribbon through the hole. *(Tie and curl the ribbon for vines.)*

Prints by the Bushel

Fall fruits and vegetables provide the finishing touches to this colorful printing project.

Supplies:

9" x 12" brown construction paper
scissors
fall fruits and vegetables (corn, small
   squash, peppers, apples, etc.)
knife (for teacher use)

1" x 9" construction paper strips
glue
12" x 18" white construction paper
shallow dishes of tempera paint

Setup:

To prepare a basket, fold the brown paper in half and cut a basket shape as shown. With the paper still folded, begin at the fold and cut slits in the basket one inch apart, stopping one inch from the outer edge. Also cut each fruit and vegetable in half or in sections to make a suitable printing surface. Allow the pieces to air dry for a few hours.

Steps:

1. Weave the paper strips through the slits in the basket.
2. Trim, adjust, and glue the strips.
3. Glue the basket to the white paper.
4. Dip the fruits and vegetables in paint and press them onto the paper. Set the painting aside to dry.

13

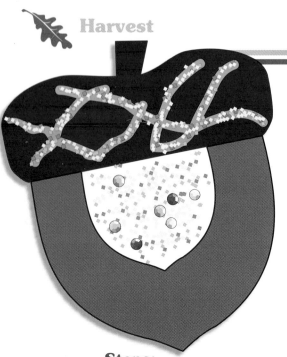

Awesome Acorn

Jazz up a fall window display with an assortment of these interesting acorns!

Supplies:

2 identical large brown
   construction paper acorns
scissors
zippered sandwich bag
1 tbsp. clear hair gel

assorted glitter and sequins
tape
glue
black construction paper
   acorn cap

Setup:

With the acorn shapes together, cut out the middle of both so that the openings are smaller than the size of the sandwich bag.

Steps:

1. Put glitter, sequins, and hair gel in the sandwich bag. *(Remove the air and seal the bag.)*
2. Press and gently squeeze the bag to distribute the contents.
3. Position the bag over the opening of one of the acorns and tape down the edges.
4. Glue the remaining acorn atop the first.
5. Decorate the acorn cap as desired.
6. Glue the cap to the acorn.

Sue Fleischmann—Preschool, Child and Family Centers of Excellence, Waukesha, WI

Salty Scarecrow

Transform a small plastic jar into this cute little scarecrow paperweight with a few simple steps!

Supplies:

small, clear plastic jar and lid
salt
powdered paint
glue
5" yellow felt circle (hair)*

4" fabric circle (hat)*
rubber band
permanent marker
small craft foam triangle (nose)
scissors

This circle size fits a 2" diameter jar lid. Adjust as needed to fit the jar you are using.

Setup:

Mix the salt and colored powdered paint until a desired color forms. Fill the jar with the mixture and glue on the lid. Prepare the five-inch circle by fringing around its edge.

Steps:

1. Stack the hat atop the hair.
2. Center the hat and hair over the jar lid and secure with a rubber band.
3. Use a marker to add eyes and a mouth.
4. Glue the nose in place.

   Sue Fleischmann—Preschool

Scarecrow Window Peeker

This fun scarecrow adds interest to a window—and there's no chance he'll scare anyone away!

Supplies:

12" x 18" construction paper (hat)
12" square of tan construction paper (head)
two 2" pink construction paper circles
   (cheeks)
two 2" white construction paper circles (eyes)
small orange construction paper triangle
   (nose)
construction paper scraps (patches)
six 1" x 5" yellow construction paper strips (hair)
scissors
glue
pencil
black marker

Setup:

Cut a hat from the 12" x 18" paper similar to the one shown.

Steps:

1. Glue the hair to each side of the head.
2. Glue the hat on the head.
3. Glue the eyes, cheeks, and nose on the head; then add other facial details using the marker.
4. Glue the patches to the hat and add details using the marker.
5. Roll the ends of the hair around a pencil to create curls.
6. Display the scarecrow, as shown, in the corner of a window.

Adapted from an idea by Cindy S. Barber—Art, Saints Cecilia and James Catholic School, Thiensville, WI

A Pile of Leaves

Jump into fall with this playful leaf project! Then attach the finished products to a bulletin board for a "tree-mendous" display.

Supplies:

scissors
full-body photograph of the child
12" x 18" fall-colored construction paper
marker
fall-colored construction paper scraps
glue
crayons

Setup:

Carefully cut out each child's outline from his photograph. Then trace a large leaf shape on a sheet of construction paper for each student.

Steps:

1. Cut out the leaf.
2. Tear scraps of paper into small pieces. Glue the pieces to the bottom of the leaf to resemble a leaf pile.
3. Glue the photo at the top of the leaf pile.
4. Draw and color any desired decorations to finish the fall scene.

Cindy S. Barber—Art, Saints Cecilia and James Catholic School, Thiensville, WI

Colorful Coffee Filters

Perk up an inexpensive coffee filter to create a colorful leaf! Use several to embellish a fall bulletin board or attach them to a window for a unique suncatcher.

Supplies:

coffee filter
food coloring in fall colors
partially filled cups of water
eyedroppers
heavy book

Setup:

Cut a leaf shape from a coffee filter. Use the food coloring to tint each cup of water a different color. Then place an eyedropper in each cup.

Steps:

1. Use the eyedroppers to drip tinted water onto the leaf. Set the leaf aside to dry.
2. Flatten the leaf by placing it under a book. *(Let it stay pressed for at least 24 hours.)*

Dawn Rolita—Gr. K, World Cup Nursery School and Kindergarten, Chappaqua, NY

Leaf Glitter

Nature supplies the glitter for these terrific trees!

Supplies:

colorful fall leaves
bowl of thinned white glue
12" x 18" white construction paper
crayons
paintbrush

Setup:

Have students tear leaves into small pieces and add them to the glue.

Steps:

1. Color a fall scene on the paper, making sure to include several trees.
2. Brush the glue mixture on and under the trees.

Jill Davis—Grs. K–1 Multiage, Kendall-Whittier Elementary, Tulsa, OK

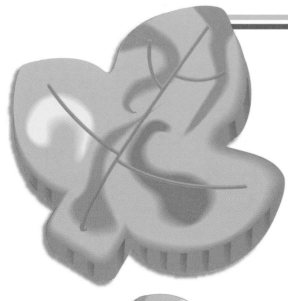

Seasonal Jewelry

This fabulous fall-inspired jewelry makes a delightful gift!

Supplies:

Crayola Model Magic modeling
   material in fall colors
small leaf-shaped cookie cutter
pin back
hot glue gun (for teacher use)

Steps:

1. Take a small piece of each color of Model Magic modeling material. Roll into a ball and then flatten to a quarter-inch thickness.
2. Use the cookie cutter to cut a leaf shape from the flattened ball. *(Dry the leaf according to the package's directions. Then hot-glue a pin back to the leaf.)*

Keely Peasner—Preschool, Midlands Kiddie Korral and Head Start, Tacoma, WA

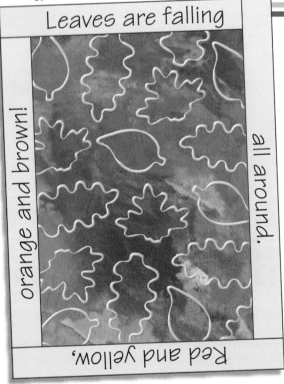

Leaves are falling

orange and brown!

all around.

Red and yellow,

Lyrical Leaf Pictures

For a project rich in fall fun, have each little one make a gleaming leaf picture! A class set of finished projects looks particularly nice as a hallway display!

Supplies:

9" x 12" white construction paper
watercolor paints
paintbrush
leaf-shaped cookie cutters*
shallow pan of gold metallic paint*
two 1" x 9" colorful paper strips, programmed as shown
two 1" x 12" colorful paper strips, programmed as shown
glue

If desired, a rubber leaf stamp and gold ink pad may be used in place of cookie cutters and metallic paint.

Steps:

1. Paint the paper with fall colors. Set the paper aside to dry. *(If the paper curls, place it under a heavy book for at least 24 hours.)*
2. Dip a cookie cutter into the metallic paint. Then print leaf shapes onto the paper, adding more paint to the cookie cutter when necessary. Set the paper aside to dry.
3. Glue the strips to the edges of the paper as shown to frame the artwork.

Cindy S. Barber—Art, Saints Cecilia and James Catholic School, Thiensville, WI

Signs of Fall

Give a hearty welcome to the fall season with this nifty sign!

Supplies:

6" x 9" cardboard
4" x 6" orange paper labeled "Welcome Fall"
glue

assorted natural objects
12" length of jute (or yarn)
tape

Setup:

Have students collect a variety of natural objects, such as twigs, acorns, pinecones, and fall leaves.

Steps:

1. Glue the sign to the cardboard.
2. Glue natural objects around the sign. Set it aside to dry.
3. Tape the jute to the back of the sign to make a hanger.

Cindy S. Barber—Art

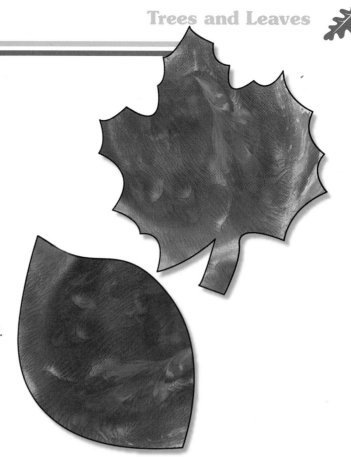

Paper Plate Spin

One, two, three! That's all it takes to make the swirling colors on these leaves!

Supplies:

2 large paper plates
2 or 3 fall-colored tempera paints
scissors

Steps:

1. Drizzle a small amount of each paint color on a plate.
2. Stack a plate on top.
3. Spin the top plate three times; then separate it from the bottom plate. Set the plates aside to dry. *(Cut a leaf shape from each plate.)*

Sue Fleischmann—Preschool, Child and Family Centers of Excellence, Waukesha, WI

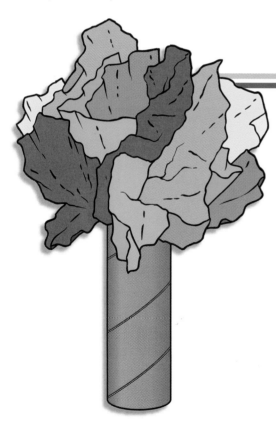

A Fall Forest

Can this project bring the beauty of fall right into your classroom? It sure can! Cover a table with green bulletin board paper. Then arrange the finished trees on the paper for a miniature fall forest display!

Supplies:

4" cardboard tube
brown tempera paint
paintbrush
several 9" x 12" sheets of fall-colored tissue paper
glue

Steps:

1. Paint the tube brown. Then allow time for the paint to dry.
2. Place glue just inside the rim of the tube.
3. Stack the sheets of tissue paper.
4. Gather the sheets in the middle and twist them together.
5. Bend the sheets at the twist.
6. Slide the twisted portion into the tube, adjusting as necessary to make it fit. Let the glue dry.
7. Fluff and crunch the tissue paper to resemble the foliage of a tree.

Sue Fleischmann—Preschool

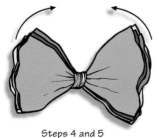

Steps 4 and 5

Paint Stick Mummy

This miniature mummy makes a cute holiday refrigerator decoration.

Supplies:

tongue depressor
tempera paint, any color (optional)
white crepe paper streamer
pom-pom (nose)

black marker
glue
adhesive magnetic tape

Steps:

1. Paint one side of the stick (optional).
2. Wrap the stick with a length of crepe paper streamer. Leave a small opening on one side (painted side, if painted) near one end. Glue the loose end in place.
3. Draw eyes in the opening with the marker.
4. Glue the nose in the opening.
5. Attach a length of magnetic tape to the back.

Sue Fleischmann—Preschool
Child and Family Centers of Excellence, Waukesha, WI

Monster Suncatcher

Scare up some fun by making this colorful monster. Then display a class set where they will catch some light. Spooky!

Supplies:

white paper
black marker
two 8" x 8" pieces of clear Con-Tact paper
tape
several 1" tissue paper squares
assorted craft supplies (foam shapes, embroidery floss, sequins, paper scraps, etc.)
scissors

Setup:

Draw an outline of a head shape on white paper no larger than 7" x 7".

Steps:

1. Place the head pattern on a flat surface and put one piece of Con-Tact paper—sticky side up—over the pattern. Tape the contact paper in place.
2. Put squares of tissue on the Con-Tact paper to fill the area inside the pattern.
3. Add embellishments to create hair, eyes, nose, and a mouth. *(Carefully place the other piece of Con-Tact paper—sticky side down—atop the project and seal the edges. Cut away the excess Con-Tact paper.)*

Sue Fleischmann—Preschool

Ghost Prints

Everyone will adore this "boo-tiful" ghost!

Supplies:

9" x 12" dark construction paper
white tempera paint
spoon
3 colored hole reinforcers

Steps:

1. Fold the paper in half; then unfold.
2. Put one spoonful of paint onto the paper.
3. Carefully refold the paper and press with your hand to spread out the paint.
4. Unfold the paper to reveal a ghost. Allow the paint to dry.
5. Attach hole reinforcers to make a face.

Jill Davis—Grs. K–1 Multiage, Kendall-Whittier Elementary, Tulsa, OK

Spooky Spoon

Serve up some fun with this simple puppet that's just perfect for little hands.

Supplies:

wooden spoon
white tissue paper
black and white curling ribbon
felt scraps
glue

Steps:

1. Place the tissue paper over the head of the spoon.
2. Tie a length of each color ribbon around the handle to secure the tissue paper.
3. Glue felt scraps to the head to make a face.

Dawn Rolita—Gr. K
World Cup Nursery School and Kindergarten
Chappaqua, NY

Handprint Spiders

This cute spider sports a personal touch! A close look reveals a student's handprints as the body.

Supplies:

black construction paper
pencil
scissors
glue
large black pom-pom
wiggle eye stickers

Setup:

Trace a child's hands (fingers and palms only—no thumbs) onto black construction paper. Cut out the handprints.

Steps:

1. Glue the handprints together with palms overlapping to make a spider. Allow the glue to dry.
2. Glue the pom-pom in the center.
3. Slightly bend the spider legs downward.
4. Add wiggle eye stickers.

Web Wonder

Line up a class set of these milk jug lid spider projects side by side for a dramatic Halloween or spider theme display.

Supplies:

9" x 12" black construction paper
white crayon
milk jug lid (body)

small pom-pom (head)
glue
glitter glue

Steps:

1. Draw a web on the black paper with the white crayon.
2. Glue the spider body and head onto the web.
3. Use glitter glue to draw eight legs extending from the body.

Cindy S. Barber—Art, Saints Cecilia and James Catholic School, Thiensville, WI

Spider Bookmark

Slip this spooky bookmark into a favorite Halloween tale to save your place!

Supplies:

2" x 7" orange construction paper
black ink pad
black fine-tip marker
hole puncher
12" length of orange yarn
plastic spider ring (optional)

Steps:

1. Press one finger onto the black ink pad; then press a pair of fingerprints onto the paper. Repeat until several sets have been made.
2. Use the fine-tip marker to add eight legs to each set of prints. *(Laminate the bookmark.)*
3. Punch a hole near one end of the bookmark.
4. Fold the yarn in half and push the folded end through the hole. Push the loose yarn ends through the loop and pull them tight. *(Tie the loose yarn ends to the ring if desired.)*

Ada Goren, Winston-Salem, NC

Mini Halloween Treat Holder

This one-of-a-kind treat will bring on a smile!

Supplies:

individual-size packaged snack or individually
   wrapped candies
cardboard tube
tape
½ sheet each of black and orange tissue paper
black and orange curling ribbon
scissors
paper scraps
glue
markers (optional)

Setup:

Push the snack into the cardboard tube. Tape each end as needed to keep the treat in the tube.

Steps:

1. With the two tissue paper colors layered, roll the tissue around the tube and secure with tape.
2. Gather the tissue ends and tie a length of each color of curling ribbon around each end.
3. Cut paper scraps and glue them to the tube to make a Halloween design or pattern. Add additional decorations with markers if desired.
4. To enjoy the treat, tear one end open.

Cute Cat Mask

Try this simple mask on for size and you're well on your way to a clever cat costume that's just perfect for trick-or-treating!

Supplies:

1" x 4" black construction paper strip
2" x 24" black tagboard
glue
pink construction paper scraps
2 black construction paper ears
scissors
3 six-inch pipe cleaners
tape

Steps:

1. Glue the end of the small paper strip to the middle of the tagboard strip.
2. Cut inner ear accents from pink paper and glue them to the ears.
3. Glue the ears to the tagboard strip.
4. Cut a nose from pink paper and glue it to the end of the small strip.
5. Tape the pipe cleaners to the back of the small strip. *(Tape the tagboard strip to fit the child's head.)*

Treat Bag Collage

Prepare for this interesting art project by collecting empty candy wrappers. The results will be rewarding!

Supplies:

two 5" x 7" black construction paper rectangles
9" x 12" construction paper
glue
5–6 candy wrappers
2 six-inch pipe cleaners
tape
holiday stickers
copy of poem (optional)

Trick-or-treat!
This is neat!
See the treats
That I can eat!

LICORICE TWISTS

PEPPERMINT PATTIE

BUBBLE GUM

gummy Critters

Steps:

1. Glue one black rectangle to the construction paper to make a bag.
2. Glue candy wrappers to the bag. Let the glue dry.
3. Bend the pipe cleaners and tape one to the top of each black rectangle to form a handle.
4. Spread a line of glue along the bottom of the wrapper-covered bag and align the remaining black rectangle atop it. Set the project aside to dry.
5. Add a title, such as "Trick-or-Treat," or a poem to the project.
6. Embellish the outer bag with holiday stickers.
7. To view the candy collage, pull the front of the bag open.

Torn-Paper Jack-o'-Lantern

Tearing and gluing are the two skills needed to make this unique jack-o'-lantern.

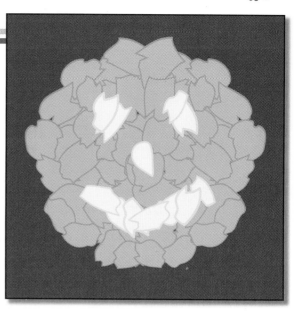

Supplies:

orange construction paper scraps
9" black construction paper square
glue
yellow construction paper scraps

Steps:

1. Tear the orange paper into small pieces.
2. Glue the orange pieces onto the black paper, overlapping the pieces. Continue until a pumpkin is formed that fills most of the paper.
3. Tear the yellow paper into small pieces.
4. Glue the yellow pieces to the pumpkin to form a face.

Jill Davis—Grs. K–1 Multiage, Kendall-Whittier Elementary, Tulsa, OK

CD Jack-o'-Lantern

This fun project finds a practical use for a recycled CD—a jolly jack-o'-lantern! Display the projects on a bulletin board by placing a pushpin through the center hole on each one!

Supplies:

recycled CD (pumpkin)
sandpaper
orange paint
paintbrush
green craft foam scraps (stem)
yellow craft foam scraps (facial features)
scissors
glue

Setup:

Lightly sand the CD to help the paint adhere.

Steps:

1. Paint the sanded side of the CD orange and allow the paint to dry.
2. Cut a stem from the green foam.
3. Glue the stem to the pumpkin.
4. Cut facial features from the yellow craft foam.
5. Glue the facial features to the pumpkin.

Cindy S. Barber—Art, Saints Cecilia and James Catholic School, Thiensville, WI

Veteran Vick

Display this windsock character as a hearty thank-you to veterans everywhere!

Supplies:

red construction paper heart
marker
9" x 12" white construction paper
sponge
shallow dishes of green and brown
   tempera paint
3" x 12" flesh-toned construction paper
crayons

glue
crepe paper streamers
stapler
hole puncher
16" length of yarn

Setup:

For each child, label a heart cutout "Thank You, Veterans!"

Steps:

1. Sponge-paint the white paper with green and brown paint. Allow time for the paint to dry.
2. Draw a face in the center of the paper strip.
3. Glue the strip to the paper as shown.
4. Glue the heart below the face.
5. Turn the paper over and glue crepe paper streamers to the bottom edge. *(Roll and then staple the prepared paper to make a cylinder. Punch two holes near the top, insert the yarn, and tie to form a hanger.)*

Sue Fleischmann—Preschool, Child and Family Centers of Excellence, Waukesha, WI

Patriotic Painting

Youngsters will have a ball making patriotic paintings in red, white, and blue!

Supplies:

small shirt box
white construction paper (sized to fit the box)
red, white, and blue tempera paint
small ball

Steps:

1. Place the paper in the box.
2. Drizzle on the paper a small amount of each color of paint.
3. Place the ball on the paper; then place the lid on the box.
4. Hold the box tightly; then roll the ball around by shaking and tilting the box.
5. Remove the painting and set it aside to dry.

Jill Davis—Grs. K–1 Multiage, Kendall-Whittier Elementary, Tulsa, OK

Colander Creations

Enrich Veterans Day with these star-spangled speckled paintings!

Supplies:

9" x 12" white construction paper
construction paper stars
tape
colander
toothbrush
shallow dishes of blue and red tempera paint

Steps:

1. Tape the star patterns to the paper.
2. Place the colander over the paper.
3. Dip the toothbrush into a dish of paint. Then rub the toothbrush on the colander over the paper.
4. Repeat the process with the second color of paint. Allow time for the paint to dry.
5. Remove the stars.

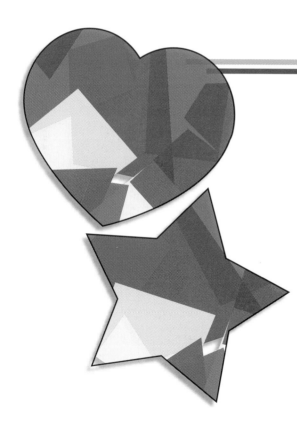

Super Suncatchers

These suncatchers are a kid-pleasing way to say "Hurray for Veterans Day!" Tape the finished projects to a window in your classroom for a patriotic display both inside and outside the classroom!

Supplies:

red, white, and blue tissue paper squares
two 9" x 12" pieces of Con-Tact paper
scissors

Setup:

Remove the backing from a sheet of Con-Tact paper and place it faceup in a work area.

Step:

Place tissue paper squares on the Con-Tact paper, overlapping the colors. *(Remove the backing from the second piece of Con-Tact paper and place it over the prepared piece. Then cut out a heart and star.)*

Jill Davis—Grs. K–1 Multiage, Kendall-Whittier Elementary, Tulsa, OK

Corn and Stuffing

There's nothing corny about this decorative corn-on-the-cob craft!

Supplies:

2 brown paper lunch bags
newspaper
string
½" squares of colored construction paper
glue
ribbon

Steps:

1. Crumple the newspaper and stuff it into each bag until the bag is about two-thirds full.
2. Squeeze each bag to mold it into a corncob shape.
3. Tie each bag securely with string about one-third of the way from the opening.
4. Gently tear the unstuffed end of the bag into strips.
5. Glue the squares in rows on the smoothest side of each corncob.
6. Tie the corncobs together with the ribbon.

Cindy S. Barber—Art, Saints Cecilia and James Catholic School, Thiensville, WI

"Shape-copia"

This bountiful harvest of shapes makes a colorful fall display!

Supplies:

brown construction paper cornucopia
construction paper cut into assorted shapes
glue

Step:

Glue a variety of shapes onto the cornucopia to resemble different fruits and vegetables.

Keely Peasner—Preschool, Midlands Kiddie Korral and Head Start, Tacoma, WA

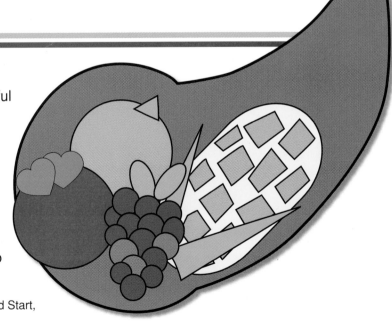

Circle of Feathers

This easy-to-make turkey adds a colorful border to any fall display.

Supplies:

8" brown construction paper circle
6" yellow construction paper circle
5" orange construction paper circle
4" red construction paper circle
5" brown construction paper peanut shape (turkey body)
construction paper scraps
scissors
glue
black marker

Steps:

1. Glue the yellow circle onto the brown circle.
2. Glue the orange circle onto the yellow circle.
3. Glue the red circle onto the orange circle.
4. Glue on the turkey body.
5. Cut out turkey feet, a beak, and a waddle from scrap paper and glue them to the turkey body.
6. Draw eyes on the turkey.

Sue Fleischmann—Preschool, Child and Family Centers of Excellence, Waukesha, WI

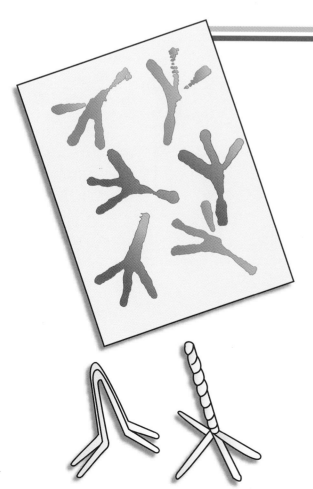

Turkey Feet Painting

Pitter, patter—these little turkey feet make interesting prints!

Supplies:

shallow dish of orange tempera paint
shallow dish of brown tempera paint
4 pipe cleaners
construction paper

Setup:

Bend and twist two pipe cleaners into a turkey foot–shaped stamper as shown. Make one stamper for each color of paint.

Steps:

1. Dip the stamper into paint.
2. Press the stamper onto the paper several times.
3. Repeat Steps 1 and 2 with a different color of paint.

Keely Peasner—Preschool, Midlands Kiddie Korral and Head Start, Tacoma, WA

Gobbling Good Recipe Holder

A recycled CD makes this terrific turkey a unique parent gift.

Supplies:

recycled CD
4" white construction paper circle
watercolor paints
paintbrushes
1¼" x 3½" brown craft foam rectangle (turkey body)
yellow craft foam scrap
washable paint pens
spring-type clothespin
recipe card
scissors
glue

Steps:

1. Paint a design on the paper circle to resemble turkey feathers. Let the paint dry.
2. Glue the circle onto the CD.
3. Glue the clothespin onto the CD as shown. Let the glue dry.
4. Glue the turkey body onto the clothespin.
5. Cut a small triangle from craft foam for the beak and glue it on the body.
6. Use paint pens to add eyes, a waddle, feathers, and feet to the body. Let the paint dry.
7. Snap the recipe card onto the turkey.

Cindy S. Barber—Art, Saints Cecilia and James Catholic School, Thiensville, WI

Turkey Mosaic

Gobble, gobble! Combine art with fine-motor skills as youngsters tear the paper needed for this colorful turkey.

Supplies:

brown construction paper turkey body
construction paper scraps
glue
scissors

Setup:

Have students tear some of the construction paper scraps into approximately one-inch pieces. If desired, have youngsters sort the scraps by color for ease of use.

Steps:

1. Glue different colors of torn paper onto the turkey body to make a desired design.
2. Cut out a beak, an eye, a waddle, and feet from scrap paper. Glue them in place.

Thankful Plate

This decorative plate is a beautiful reminder of Thanksgiving.

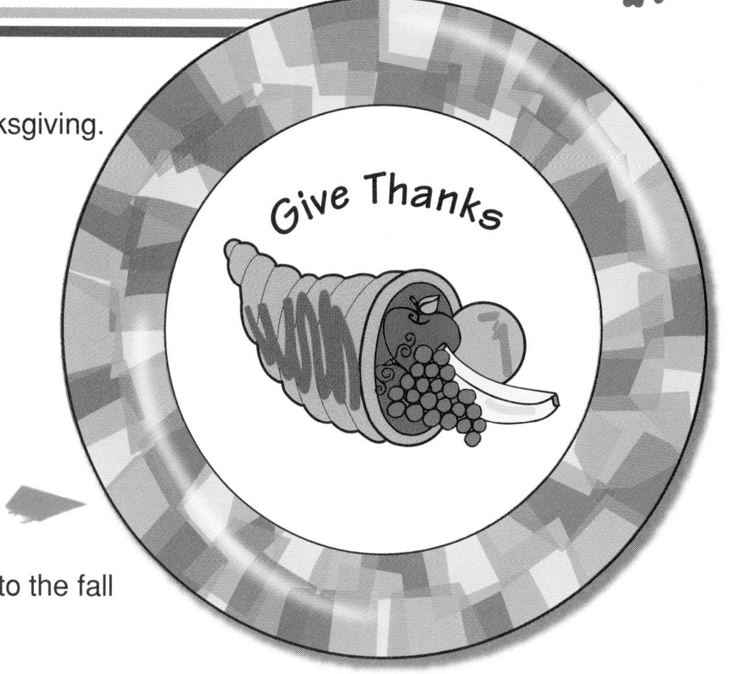

Supplies:

9" clear plastic plate
fall coloring picture
1" tissue paper squares in orange, red, and yellow
5 ¾" tagboard circle template
gloss-finish Mod Podge mixture
paintbrush
crayons
scissors

Setup:

Add a Thanksgiving phrase, such as "Give Thanks," to the fall picture.

Steps:

1. Color the picture.
2. Trace the circle template around the picture and then cut along the line.
3. Lay the plate facedown and brush the Mod Podge mixture onto the center circle area of it.
4. Lay the picture facedown on top of the Mod Podge mixture. Then brush the back of the picture with the Mod Podge mixture.
5. Brush the Mod Podge mixture onto the rim of the plate.
6. Cover the rim of the plate with tissue paper squares. Press down slightly to flatten.
7. Carefully brush the Mod Podge mixture on top of the tissue paper. Let it dry.

Cindy S. Barber—Art, Saints Cecilia and James Catholic School, Thiensville, WI

Handy Thank-You

Put your hands together for this note of thanksgiving.

Supplies:

6" x 9" construction paper   scissors
markers   crayons

Steps:

1. Place your hands, with thumbs together, on a sheet of paper. Have a partner trace your hands. *(Cut out the tracing.)*
2. Write a thank-you message on the cutout, and then draw a picture to illustrate it.
3. If desired, fold the hands in half to make a card.

Keely Peasner—Preschool, Midlands Kiddie Korral and Head Start
Tacoma, WA

I'm thankful for Mom and Dad.

Heartfelt Turkey

This special holiday card has sentiments straight from the heart.

Supplies:

9" x 12" construction paper
4" brown construction paper heart (turkey body)
craft feathers
glue
2" peanut-shaped brown construction paper cutout
   (turkey head)
yellow construction paper diamond (beak)
markers
copy of poem

Steps:

1. Fold the sheet of paper in half to make a card.
2. Glue the heart upside down on the front of the card. Arrange the feathers behind the top of the heart. Glue all the pieces in place.
3. Glue the turkey head onto the middle of the body.
4. Glue on the beak.
5. Draw on eyes, a waddle, and turkey feet. Let dry.
6. Glue the poem inside the card.
7. Write "Love" and sign your name at the bottom of the card.

Sue Fleischmann—Preschool, Child and Family Centers of Excellence, Waukesha, WI

I made a little turkey
For Thanksgiving Day
To wish you lots of love
In a heartfelt way.

This funny little turkey
Is made of many parts.
Then I added lots of love
Straight from my heart!

Happy Thanksgiving!

Love,
Jasmine

❄ Winter ❄

Pretty Snowpals!

A jumbo hole puncher is the key to these lacy-looking snowpals! Attach the completed pictures to a bulletin board for a festive winter-themed display!

Supplies:

doilies
jumbo hole puncher
hole puncher
white, black, and orange construction paper scraps
9" x 12" blue construction paper
glue

Setup:

Hole-punch a supply of jumbo circles from the doilies. Also hole-punch a supply of small black paper dots.

Setup:

1. Tear pieces of white paper (snow) and glue them to the bottom of the blue paper.
2. Glue trios of doily circles (snowpals) above the snow.
3. Glue paper dot eyes and buttons on each snowpal.
4. Tear orange paper noses. Glue one on each snowpal.
5. Tear white paper snowflakes. Glue them above the snowpals.

Angie Kutzer—Gr. K, Garrett Elementary, Mebane, NC

Snowstorm

Reveal a snowy surprise with a wash of blue paint! When the projects are dry, invite each student to take his picture home to share with his family!

Supplies:

manila drawing paper
white crayon
thinned blue tempera paint
paintbrush
glitter glue (optional)

Steps:

1. Use a white crayon to draw a snowstorm on the paper.
2. Brush paint over the entire paper to reveal the drawing. Then set the painting aside to dry.
   (If desired, when the paint is dry, have each student embellish his painting with glitter glue.)

Angie Kutzer—Gr. K

Fluffy Snowflakes

These hanging snowflakes make your classroom look like a winter wonderland! To hang the finished flakes, shape one of the pipe cleaner ends into a loop. Tie a length of fishing line to the loop, and then hang the snowflake from your classroom ceiling!

Supplies:

3 pipe cleaners	shallow dish of glue
aluminum foil	spoon
cotton balls	glitter

Setup:

To make a snowflake, gather the pipe cleaners into a bundle. Twist the center of the bundle and then spread out the pipe cleaners.

Steps:

1. Lay the snowflake on a sheet of aluminum foil.
2. Dip cotton balls into the glue, and press them firmly onto the pipe cleaners until a desired effect is achieved.
3. Use a spoon to drizzle glue onto the cotton balls.
4. Sprinkle glitter over the glue. Allow time for the glue to dry.
5. Peel the snowflake off the foil.

Betty Silkunas—Gr. K, Lower Gwynedd Elementary, Ambler, PA

Is It Warm in Here?

This grin-inducing snowpal will risk looking a bit melted to stay in your warm and cozy classroom! Display the finished projects on a bulletin board titled "Is It Warm in Here?"

Supplies:

nonmenthol shaving cream	12" x 18" blue construction paper
white glue	orange, black, and brown
large bowl	construction paper
mixing spoon	scissors

Setup:

Mix equal parts shaving cream and white glue in the bowl. Spoon a large dollop of the mixture onto a sheet of blue paper for each child.

Steps:

1. Use your fingers to spread the mixture on the paper to form a snowpal.
2. Cut eyes, a nose, arms, buttons, and any other desired decorations from the construction paper. Then gently press them onto the mixture. *(Allow the project to dry for at least 3 days.)*

Chalene McGrath—Special Education PreK, Discovery School, Brigham City, UT

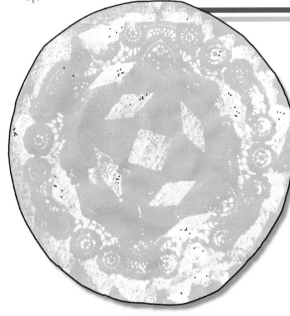

Doily Snowflake

This elegant snowflake is delightfully simple!

Supplies:

blue construction paper
large paper doily
tape

shallow dish of white tempera paint
sponge
scissors

Setup:

Lightly tape a doily to the paper.

Steps:

1. Use the sponge to dab paint on the doily, taking care to get paint between the spaces.
2. Remove the doily. Allow time for the paint to dry.
3. Cut out the snowflake.

Gail Marsh—Preschool and Pre-Kindergarten, St. Mark's Lutheran School, Eureka, MO

Cool Color Collage

There's no doubt about it! This colorful collage looks really cool! Display a class set on a wall for all to enjoy.

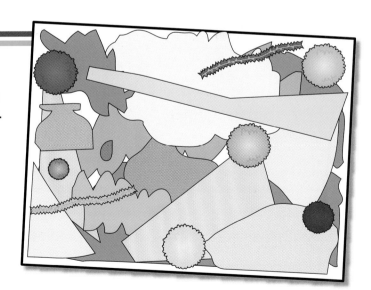

Supplies:

white construction paper
assorted art supplies in various shades of blue, green, and purple

scissors
glue

Setup:

Explain that colors can be thought of as warm or cool. Green, blue, and purple are cool colors and might make people think of a chilly winter's day.

Step:

Glue an assortment of art supplies to the paper.

Beth Allison—Preschool–Gr. 5 Art; Austinville, Benjamin Davis, and Frances Nungester Elementary Schools; Decatur, AL

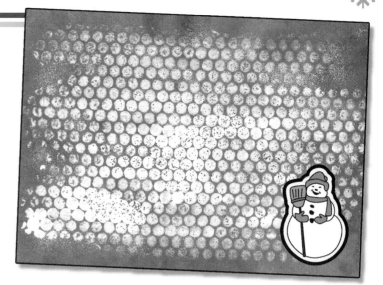

Snowballs Galore

Youngsters bubble over with excitement when they participate in this print-making activity!

Supplies:

9" x 12" piece of bubble wrap
white tempera paint
glitter
paintbrush
9" x 12" blue construction paper
snowman sticker (optional)

Setup:

Mix glitter into the paint.

Steps:

1. Brush paint on the bubble wrap.
2. Place a sheet of paper over the bubble wrap. Then press on the paper to transfer the paint.
3. Lift up the paper. Set it aside to dry.
4. Stick a snowman sticker among the snowballs if desired.

Beth Allison—Preschool–Gr. 5 Art; Austinville, Benjamin Davis, and Frances Nungester Elementary Schools; Decatur, AL

Overlapping Icicles

This art project brings the beauty of icicles indoors! Hang the projects in a row to give the appearance of a never-ending icy display.

Supplies:

12" x 18" blue construction paper
various shades of blue construction
   paper and tissue paper
white construction paper

aluminum foil
scissors
glue

Steps:

1. Cut or tear the paper and aluminum foil to resemble icicles.
2. Glue overlapping icicles on the 12" x 18" sheet of paper. Set the project aside to dry.

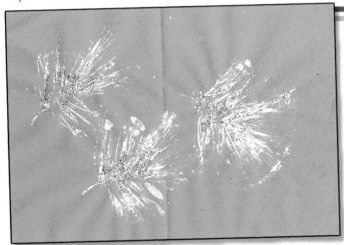

Brrr Branches

Make an impression on your youngsters with frosty pine branch prints!

Supplies:

12" x 18" green construction paper
small pine tree branch
white tempera paint
paintbrush
iridescent glitter (optional)

Steps:

1. Brush paint on one side of the pine branch.
2. Lay the branch on the paper and press down firmly.
3. Lift up the branch. Then repeat the process until a desired effect is achieved.
4. If desired, sprinkle glitter over the wet paint. Shake off the excess glitter and set the project aside to dry.

Terrific Templates

For first-time template users, this snowpal is the tops!

Supplies:

3 large heavy-duty paper plates
scissors
12" x 18" construction paper
white and colored chalk
hairspray (for teacher use)

Setup:

Make a template for each section of the snowman by cutting a different-size circle from the center of each paper plate.

Steps:

1. Use white chalk to trace each template onto the paper to form a snowman.
2. Color in the circles to resemble a snowpal.
3. Use colored chalk to add snowpal details, such as eyes, a nose, and arms. *(Spray the picture with hairspray to keep the chalk from smudging.)*

Beth Allison—Preschool–Gr. 5 Art; Austinville, Benjamin Davis, and Frances Nungester Elementary Schools; Decatur, AL

A Snowy Scene

Salty tempera paint gives this nighttime scene a unique texture! When the projects are dry, display them at students' eye level so they are able to touch this appealing paint.

Supplies:

12" x 18" black construction paper
white tempera paint
1 c. measuring cup
liquid starch
tablespoon
table salt
paintbrush
colorful tempera
   paint (optional)

Setup:

To make salty tempera paint, mix one cup white paint, two tablespoons salt, and one tablespoon liquid starch.

Steps:

1. Paint a snow scene on the paper with the prepared salt paint.
2. Add details with tempera paint, if desired. Set the painting aside to dry.

Fancy Snowpal

Little ones strengthen their fine-motor skills when they make this adorable snowpal!

Supplies:

2 large paper plates
hole puncher
two 16" lengths of ribbon
tape
glue
colorful construction paper
scissors

Setup:

Punch an even number of holes around the edge of each plate. Tape a ribbon to each plate to keep it from pulling through the holes while lacing.

Steps:

1. Lace each ribbon through the holes of a plate. *(When each child is finished, cut off any extra ribbon and tape down the loose ends.)*
2. Glue the plates back to back to resemble a snowpal.
3. Cut a hat and other details from construction paper and then glue them to the snowpal.

39

Clever Candle Prints

Celebrate Hanukkah with this creative candle printmaking project.

Supplies:

3 candles with various textures, such as
   birthday candles
construction paper
shallow dishes of blue, light blue, and white
   tempera paint
paper towels

Steps:

1. Dip one candle into one color of paint.
2. Press the candle onto the construction paper several times. *(Help the student use a paper towel to wipe his hands after using each color of paint.)*
3. Repeat Steps 1 and 2 with each remaining color of paint, overlapping prints if desired. Let the paint dry.

Coramarie Marinan—Gr. K, Howe School
Green Bay, WI

Night Light

Shed light on this project and add a candle twist to familiar wax-resist painting.

Supplies:

white candle
yellow construction paper
diluted black tempera paint
paintbrush

Steps:

1. Use a candle to draw a picture on the paper. *(Explain to youngsters that the wax will resist the paint and their drawing will magically appear!)*
2. Brush paint over the picture. Let the paint dry.

Coramarie Marinan—Gr. K

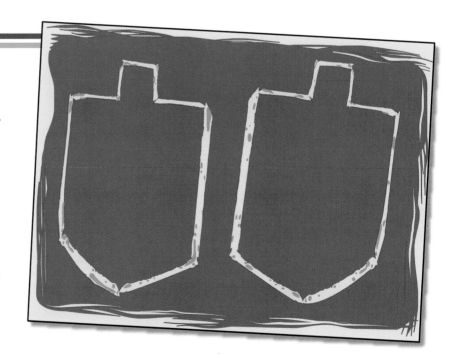

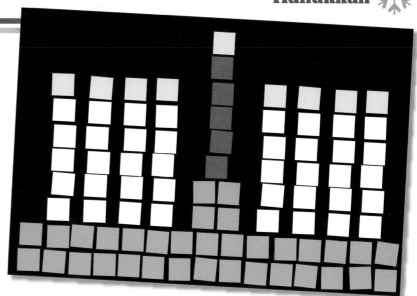

Mosaic Menorah

Put all the pieces together on this art center project to create a dramatic display of color and light.

Supplies:

12" x 18" black construction paper
1" construction paper squares (9 yellow, 5 purple, 34 blue, 40 white)
glue

Setup:

Display the finished sample for use as a reference. Give the child the required number of squares in each color.

Steps:

1. Glue two rows of 15 blue squares along the horizontal bottom of the paper to make a candle base.
2. Glue four blue squares in the middle of the base. Glue five purple squares above those to create the shammash.
3. Glue five white squares vertically onto the base to create a candle. Make seven more white candles in the same manner.
4. Glue one yellow square above each candle to make a flame.

Angie Kutzer—Gr. K, Garrett Elementary, Mebane, NC

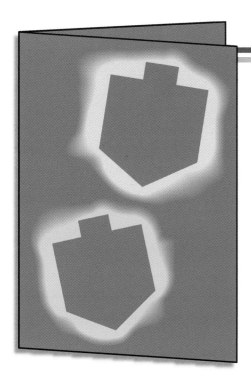

Chalky Greeting

A smudge or smear on this holiday greeting card is expected!

Supplies:

9" x 12" construction paper
colored chalk
tagboard holiday template, such as a dreidel or star

Steps:

1. With the paper horizontally positioned, fold it in half to make a card.
2. Use chalk to trace the template onto the front of the card.
3. Hold the template in place with one hand. Use the other hand to smudge the chalk outward. Remove the pattern.
4. Repeat Steps 2 and 3 as space allows.

Jingle Joy

Ring in the sound of the season with a sparkling bell that's perfect for classroom plays or musicals.

Supplies:

foam cup
giant jingle bell
pipe cleaner

glitter
gallon-size resealable plastic bag
glue stick

Setup:

Pour glitter into the bag.

Steps:

1. Spread glue over the outside of the cup.
2. Place the cup in the bag and seal it. Shake the bag until the cup is covered with glitter. Remove the cup from the bag and let the glue dry.
3. Thread the jingle bell onto the pipe cleaner. Twist the pipe cleaner to secure the jingle bell. *(Carefully poke the pipe cleaner ends through the inside bottom of the cup. Twist the ends together to form a loop.)*

Gail Marsh—Preschool and Pre-Kindergarten, St. Mark's Lutheran School, Eureka, MO

Peppermint Painting

This big peppermint project makes a sweet-smelling classroom decoration!

Supplies:

14" x 24" piece of white bulletin
   board paper
red tempera paint
paintbrush
peppermint extract

newspaper
tape
2 pipe cleaners
two 12" lengths of red yarn

Steps:

1. Lay the bulletin board paper on a flat surface.
2. Paint red stripes on the paper. Let it dry.
3. Lay the paper painted-side down. *(Place one drop of peppermint extract on the paper.)*
4. Place crumpled newspaper on top of the paper and roll the paper into a tube shape (with the newspaper inside the tube).
5. Secure the tube with tape.
6. Pinch one end shut and secure it with a pipe cleaner; then repeat with the unfinished end to make a candy shape.
7. Tie yarn around each end to cover each pipe cleaner.

Shimmering Ornament

Capture the sparkle and shine of the season with these oversize ornaments.

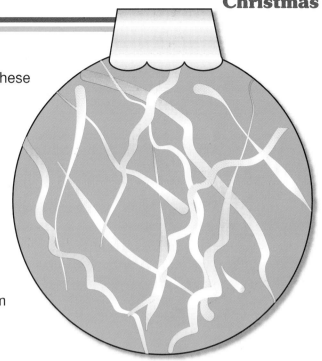

Supplies:

aluminum foil
scissors
8" construction paper circle
waxed paper
squeeze bottles of gold and silver tempera paints
glue

Setup:

Cut a large ornament hanger shape from aluminum foil for each child.

Steps:

1. Place the paper circle on a square of waxed paper.
2. Drizzle silver and gold paint onto the paper. Let it dry.
3. Glue the foil hanger at the top of the ornament. Let it dry. *(Laminate the ornament if desired.)*

Ada Goren, Winston-Salem, NC

Marbleized Candy Cane

This holiday treat looks good enough to eat!

Supplies:

shallow rectangular pan
liquid starch
3 craft sticks
red and white acrylic paints, thinned
9" white construction paper candy cane

newspaper
newsprint
10" red construction
  paper candy cane
glue

Setup:

Partially fill the pan with liquid starch.

Steps:

1. Dip a craft stick into the red paint and then drizzle it onto the liquid starch.
2. Repeat Step 1 with the white paint.
3. Gently swirl the paint with a craft stick.
4. Carefully lay the white candy cane on top of the mixture.
5. Carefully lift the candy cane out of the pan and lay it on newspaper. Blot the candy cane with newsprint to remove excess starch. Let the paint dry.
6. Glue the painted candy cane to the red candy cane.

Dawn Rolita—Gr. K, World Cup Nursery School and Kindergarten, Chappaqua, NY

Wrap It Up!

Science exploration and art combine to make this festive wrapping paper.

Supplies:

food coloring   eye droppers
vegetable oil   rectangular pan
several small plastic containers   water
white copy paper

Setup:

Partially fill several containers with water. As students observe, add several drops of a different color of food coloring to each container and mix well. Then pour oil into a separate plastic container.

Steps:

1. Lay the paper on a flat surface.
2. Use eye droppers to place several drops of each different-colored water on the paper.
3. Use an eyedropper to drip several drops of oil on the paper, near the colored water droplets.
4. Carefully lift the paper and hold it over the pan to allow the excess water and oil to drip into the pan. *(The water and oil will run together as it runs down the paper. The two liquids won't mix, but will make interesting designs.)* Set the paper aside to dry.
5. Use the wrapping paper to wrap a special holiday present.

Beth Allison—Preschool–Gr. 5 Art; Austinville, Benjamin Davis, and
Frances Nungester Elementary Schools; Decatur, AL

Torn-Paper Ornament

Tear it up! Exercise fine-motor skills as youngsters prepare paper for this easy-to-make holiday decoration.

Supplies:

holiday wrapping paper
small paper plate
glue
ribbon
access to a hole puncher

Steps:

1. Tear the paper into small pieces.
2. Glue the torn paper on the paper plate. Let it dry.
3. Punch a hole at the top of the plate and thread a ribbon through it. Tie the ribbon to make an ornament hanger.

Beth Allison—Preschool–Gr. 5 Art

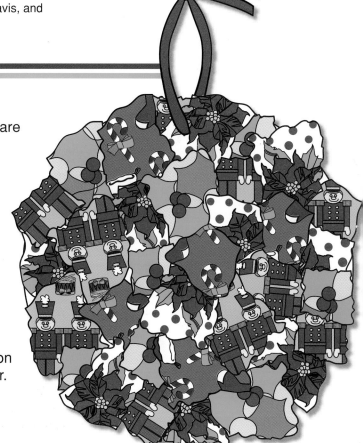

44

Lovely Angel Banner

All your little angels will shine as they make this picture-perfect banner for a loved one.

Supplies:

child's photo (large-size headshot)
scissors
9" x 12" white construction paper
red, yellow, and flesh tone
    tempera paints

glue
gold or silver glitter glue
yellow marker

Setup:

Trim each child's photograph as shown.

Steps:

1. Make one upside-down red handprint on the middle of the paper to make an angel body. Let it dry.
2. Make two upside-down yellow handprints close to the body to make angel wings. Let the paint dry.
3. Fingerpaint two red arms. Let the paint dry.
4. Add flesh-tone fingerprints to resemble angel hands.
5. Glue on the photo.
6. Trace each wing with glitter glue. Add a glitter glue halo above the head. Let the glue dry.
7. Use the marker to make stars above the angel.
8. Write "I love you this much!" below the angel. *(If desired, laminate each banner.)*

Stacy Wingen—Gr. K, Howard Elementary, Howard, SD

I love you this much.

"Tree-rific" Greeting!

Here's a simple greeting card that's as much fun to make as it is to give!

Supplies:

stalk of celery
knife (for teacher use only)
9" x 12" red construction paper
glue

5" green triangle (tree)
white or silver tempera paint
marker

Setup:

Cut the end off each stalk of celery to make a flat surface for printing. Allow a few hours for the celery to air dry.

Steps:

1. Fold the red paper in half to make a card.
2. Glue the tree onto the front of the card.
3. Dip the celery into paint and make a row of prints on the tree to resemble garland.
4. Repeat Step 3 to make several rows of garland on the tree. Let the paint dry.
5. Add a greeting and a signature to the inside of the card.

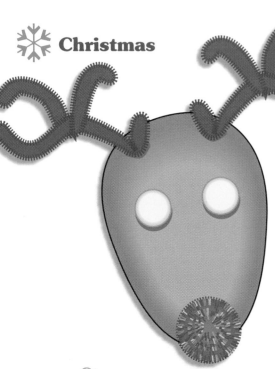

Really Rudolph Magnet

This red-nosed refrigerator magnet will capture everyone's attention!

Supplies:

red, yellow, and blue Crayola Model Magic modeling compound
brown pipe cleaner, cut in fourths
red sparkle pom-pom
craft glue
adhesive magnetic tape

Setup:

Give each child a golf ball–size portion of each color of modeling compound.

Steps:

1. Roll two small yellow eyes and set aside.
2. Knead the remaining yellow, red, and blue together to create a brown ball.
3. Form an oval shape and then gently press it on a table to flatten one side.
4. Press the eyes onto the oval.
5. Twist two pieces of pipe cleaner together to form an antler. Repeat with the two remaining pipe cleaner pieces.
6. Stick the antlers into the reindeer head.
7. Glue on a pom-pom nose. Let the glue dry.
8. Attach the magnetic tape to the back of the reindeer.

Angie Kutzer—Gr. K, Garrett Elementary, Mebane, NC

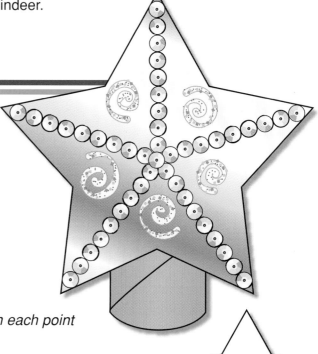

Tree Topper

This shimmering star puts the finishing touch on any tree.

Supplies:

gold or silver tempera paint
paintbrush
9" white tagboard star
pencil

glue
sequins
glitter glue
4" cardboard tube

Steps:

1. Paint the star and let it dry. (Draw a light pencil line from each point to the center.)
2. Trace the lines on the star with glue.
3. Place sequins on the glue.
4. Use glitter glue to decorate the star as desired.
5. Glue the tube onto the back of the star as shown. Hold in place until the glue holds.
6. Place the tube over a branch on the tree.

Pretty Pink Poinsettia

These pink poinsettias make a serene seasonal display.

Supplies:

pink and green bulletin board paper
small yellow pom-poms
small white paper plate
glue

Steps:

1. Tear 12 to 15 petals from the pink paper.
2. Glue a layer of petals onto the plate to form a flower.
3. Tear four or five leaves from the green paper.
4. Glue the leaves among the petals.
5. Glue another layer of petals onto the plate.
6. Glue several yellow pom-poms in the middle of the flower. Allow the glue to dry.

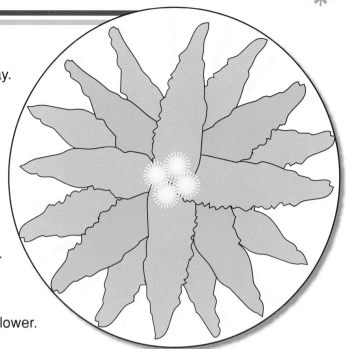

Paper-Punch Gift Bag

Engage fine-motor skills to create this festive gift bag.

Supplies:

white lunch bag
shaped paper punch
pencil
construction paper scraps
holiday cookie cutters
scissors
glue
glitter glue
yellow tissue paper

Steps:

1. With the bag flat, punch shapes along both edges of the bag.
2. Trace several cookie cutter shapes onto construction paper.
3. Cut out the shapes.
4. Glue the shapes on the front of the bag.
5. Decorate with glitter glue. Let it dry.
6. Tuck a sheet of yellow tissue paper inside the bag to highlight the punched shapes.

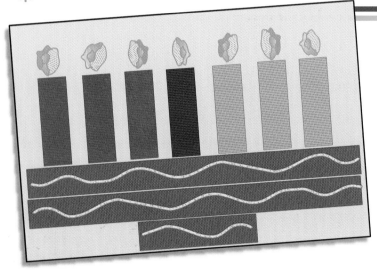

Crepe Paper Kinara

This kinara is sure to enrich a celebration of Kwanzaa!

Supplies:

12" x 18" construction paper
one 8" strip of brown crepe paper
two 17" strips of brown crepe paper
three 5" strips of red crepe paper (red candles)
one 5" strip of black crepe paper (black candle)
three 5" strips of green crepe paper (green candles)
7 yellow crepe paper squares (flames)
gold glitter glue

Steps:

1. Glue the short brown strip to the bottom of the paper.
2. Glue the two long brown strips above the small strip.
3. Glue the black candle in the center.
4. Glue three red candles on the left-hand side.
5. Glue three green candles on the right-hand side.
6. Crumple the flames and then glue each one to the top of a candle.
7. Draw wavy lines with glitter glue on each brown strip. Set the project aside to dry.

A Joyful Noise

Celebrate the creative focus of Kwanzaa with a tambourine that little hands love to rattle and shake! Encourage children to shake their tambourines as you sing or play a recording of music.

Supplies:

aluminum pie tin
black, red, and green construction paper scraps
glue
hole puncher
3 black pipe cleaners
3 large jingle bells
red and green curling ribbon

Steps:

1. Glue paper scraps to the inside of the tin. *(Hole-punch six holes around the edge of the tin. Thread each bell onto a different pipe cleaner. Insert an end of a pipe cleaner into every other hole and then tightly twist together the ends of each pipe cleaner.)*
2. Tie lengths of curling ribbon to the remaining holes.

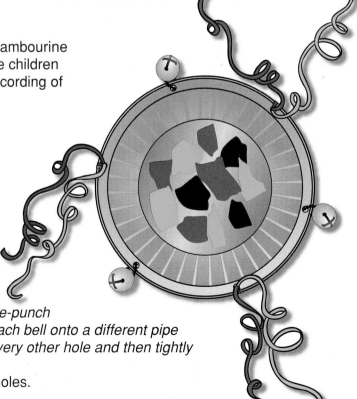

Betty Silkunas—Gr. K, Lower Gwynedd Elementary, Ambler, PA

A Marvelous *Mkeka*

Youngsters use this unique painting method to make a colorful mat called an *mkeka!* (See the idea below for an extension of this project.)

Supplies:

12" x 18" brown construction paper
shallow pans of red, green, and black tempera paint
three 7" lengths of yarn
3 clothespins
scissors

Setup:

Clip an end of each length of yarn in a clothespin.

Steps:

1. Pick up a length of yarn by the attached clothespin and dip the yarn in a dish of paint.
2. Drag the yarn across the paper, pausing to add more paint to the yarn when needed.
3. Repeat the process with each color of paint, using a different length of yarn each time. Set the mat aside to dry.
4. Use scissors to fringe the edges of the mat.

Angie Kutzer—Gr. K, Garrett Elementary, Mebane, NC

Crafty Corn

For each child in a family, an ear of corn, or *muhindi,* should be placed on the mkeka. Have each child glue ears of this crafty corn on his mat from the idea above!

Supplies:

6" strip of yellow crepe paper (corncob)
two 4" strips of green crepe paper (husks)
raffia (silk)

Steps:

1. Trim the yellow strip to resemble a corncob. Then glue the cob to the mat.
2. Glue a small amount of silk to the corncob.
3. Glue the husks to either side of the corncob as shown.
4. Add supplies and repeat Steps 1–3 for each child in your family.

Angie Kutzer—Gr. K

Quiet Confetti Popper

Pop, pop, pop! This project puts youngsters' fine-motor skills in motion and produces a sparkling popper. Send each child home with one to pop open at a New Year's celebration!

Supplies:

shaped paper punchers	spoon
construction paper scraps	small stickers (with
bowl	backing)
6" x 12" aluminum foil	curling ribbon
4½" cardboard tube	markers
tape	

Steps:

1. Use the paper punches to make an assortment of construction paper confetti in the bowl.
2. Roll the foil around the tube and secure it with tape.
3. Twist the foil on one end of the tube to seal it.
4. Spoon the confetti into the open end of the tube. Add a few stickers (with backing) to the tube and then twist the end closed.
5. Tie a piece of ribbon around each end of the tube.
6. Write the year on the tube. Then decorate the tube with markers and additional stickers.

Beverly G. McCormick—Gr. K, East Brainerd Elementary, Chattanooga, TN

Nifty Noisemaker

Celebrate the new year with a jingle from this water bottle noisemaker.

Supplies:

permanent marker
16 oz. empty water bottle and cap
acrylic paints
paintbrushes
small bells (for teacher use)
hot glue gun (for teacher use)
curling ribbon

Steps:

1. Write your name on the bottom of the bottle with a permanent marker.
2. Paint the outside of the bottle as desired. Let it dry. *(Pour the bells inside the bottle and hot-glue the cap onto it.)*
3. Write the year on the bottle.
4. Tie several pieces of ribbon around the neck of the bottle.

Bangle Bracelet

Start the new year off with a bang! A "bang-le," that is! This decorative project can be worn to usher in the new year!

Supplies:

colorful plastic drinking straws
scissors
Crayola Model Magic modeling compound
8" pipe cleaner
permanent marker

Setup:

Cut the straws into ¾-inch pieces.

Steps:

1. Roll four small balls of modeling compound.
2. Thread two straw pieces onto the pipe cleaner.
3. Thread one ball followed by one straw piece onto the pipe cleaner; repeat for each remaining ball.
4. Add one or two more straw pieces to fill the pipe cleaner.
5. Twist the ends of the pipe cleaner together, and then thread the resulting end through a straw piece on the bracelet to secure it.
6. Flatten each ball to make a bead. Then use a permanent marker to write each number in the year on a separate bead. Let it dry.

Angie Kutzer—Gr. K, Garrett Elementary, Mebane, NC

New Year's Numbers

Handy number sponges make this festive headband as much fun to create as it is to wear!

Supplies:

number-shaped sponges (for the new year)
tempera paint
3" x 18" poster board strip (headband)
pom-poms
glitter glue
glue
stapler

Steps:

1. Dip each number in paint and press the new year onto the headband. Let the paint dry.
2. Decorate the headband with pom-poms and glitter glue. Let it dry. *(Fit the headband to the child's head and then staple the ends together.)*

Adapted from an idea by Betty Silkunas—Gr. K, Lower Gwynedd Elementary, Ambler, PA

A Handsome Headband

Celebrate Martin Luther King Jr.'s message of peace with these wearable reminders.

Supplies:

sentence strip
four hand cutouts in a variety of skin tones
glue
1½" x 5" paper sign labeled "The Future Is in Our Hands"
stapler

Steps:

1. Glue the hands to the center of the sentence strip in an overlapping pattern.
2. Glue the sign on top of the hands. Allow time for the glue to dry. *(Staple the headband to fit the child's head.)*

Angie Kutzer—Gr. K, Garrett Elementary, Mebane, NC

A Friendship Parade

Youngsters emphasize the importance of friendship with these extra large paintings. Have children carry the paintings and wear the headbands from the idea above for a parade celebrating Martin Luther King Jr.

Supplies:

large bulletin board paper heart
tempera paints
paintbrushes

Step:

Paint on the heart a picture of yourself and a friend doing an enjoyable activity. *(If desired, have each student dictate a sentence about her picture, and write her words under the painting.)*

Beth Allison—Preschool–Gr. 5 Art
Austinville, Benjamin Davis, and Frances Nungester Elementary Schools
Decatur, AL

My friend is Heather. We play catch and eat pizza together.

Darling Dove

Little ones will enjoy seeing this flock of peaceful doves hanging around the classroom!

Supplies:

large paper plate (body)
black marker
scissors
yellow tempera paint
paintbrush
large paper plate half, cut in half (wings)
glue
hole puncher
yarn
small twig with leaves (olive branch)

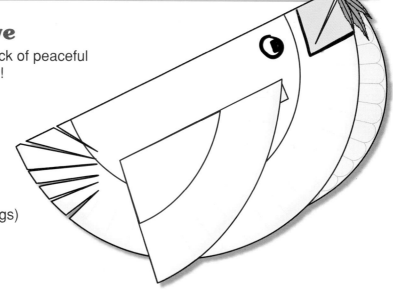

Setup:

For each child, fold a plate in half. Draw a beak and eye on both sides of the fold.

Steps:

1. Unfold the plate and cut several slits at one end of the fold line to represent tail feathers. Then refold the plate.
2. Paint the beak yellow on each side of the fold. Let the paint dry.
3. Bend a straight edge of each wing to create a small flap for gluing.
4. Place glue on the flap and then glue the wing to the body, holding the wing in place for several seconds. Repeat for the second wing. Allow the glue to dry.
5. Cut a slit for the bird's beak. Slide the olive branch into the slit. *(Hole-punch the top of the dove. Thread yarn through the hole and then suspend the dove from the ceiling.)*

Hand in hand across the land,
For Martin's dream we choose to stand.
We say it loud; we say it clear—
Peace and love throughout the year!

Peace and Love

Spotlight this petite poem with a lovely heart!

Supplies:

white tagboard
squares of tissue paper in a variety of skin tones
shallow dish of thinned glue
paintbrush
copy of the poem shown

scissors
glue

Steps:

1. Brush a thin layer of glue over the tagboard.
2. Place tissue paper squares on the glue.
3. Brush another layer of glue over the squares. Allow time for the glue to dry. *(Cut a heart shape from the tagboard.)*
4. Glue the poem to the center of the heart.

Shandella Chapman—Three- and Four-Year-Olds
Butte County Head Start, Oroville, CA

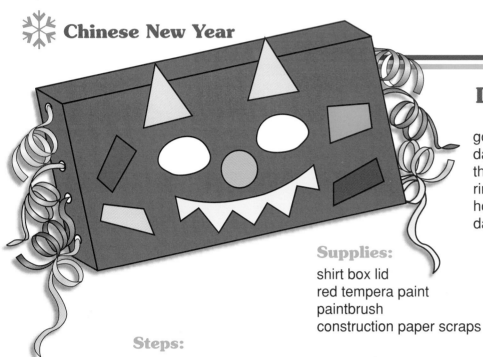

Dancing Dragon Mask

Youngsters will have a roaringly good time when they perform a dragon dance with these colorful masks! When the masks are ready, play a tambourine or drum and have each student hold his mask up to his face as he dances to the beat!

Supplies:

shirt box lid
red tempera paint
paintbrush
construction paper scraps

scissors
glue
hole puncher
curling ribbon

Steps:

1. Paint the outside of the lid red. Allow time for the paint to dry. *(Cut eyeholes in the lid.)*
2. Cut and then glue construction paper to the lid to add a nose, a mouth, and any desired decorations. Allow time for the glue to dry. *(Hole-punch the sides of the mask and tie curling ribbon through each hole.)*

Beth Allison—Preschool–Gr. 5 Art; Austinville, Benjamin Davis, and
Frances Nungester Elementary Schools; Decatur, AL

Bright Lanterns

Decorative lanterns are part of the Chinese New Year season. Have youngsters make these fancy lanterns to hang around the classroom!

Supplies:

12" x 18" yellow construction paper
red crayon
scissors
stapler
red cellophane

Setup:

Cut a 2" x 18" strip from the paper to use as a handle for the lantern.

Steps:

1. Use the red crayon to draw a Chinese New Year picture on the paper.
2. Fold the paper in half lengthwise. Then, starting from the folded side of the paper, cut several slits. *(Unfold the paper, roll it into a cylinder, and staple the edges together. Staple the handle to the top of the cylinder.)*
3. Crumple a piece of cellophane and stuff it in the center of the lantern.

Dazzling Dragon

Curling ribbon and glitter make this Chinese New Year's dragon simply dazzling!

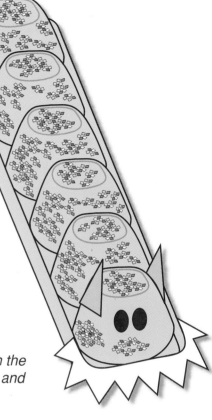

Supplies:

row of a foam egg carton,
  cleaned and sanitized (body)
green tempera paint
white glue
paintbrush
glitter
scissors

green construction paper (ears)
white construction paper (teeth)
black permanent marker
hole puncher
curling ribbon

Setup:

To make paint that adheres to foam, mix two parts glue with one part tempera paint.

Steps:

1. Paint the egg carton green. Then sprinkle glitter on the wet paint. Allow time for the paint to dry.
2. Cut ears and teeth and then glue them to the dragon.
3. Draw eyes with the black marker. *(To make a tail for the dragon, hole-punch the end of the carton. Thread several lengths of curling ribbon through the hole and tie them in a knot under the dragon.)*

Angie Kutzer—Gr. K, Garrett Elementary, Mebane, NC

Noodle Bowl

During the Chinese New Year, people eat bowls of noodles, which symbolize long life. Have youngsters make these crafty noodle bowls. Then display them on a bulletin board with the title "We Wish You a Long Life!"

Supplies:

lengths of white yarn
shallow pan of liquid starch
9" square of aluminum foil

blue construction paper bowl
9" x 12" red construction paper
glue

Steps:

1. Dip a length of yarn into the liquid starch. Then slide the yarn between two fingers to remove the excess starch.
2. Lay the yarn on the foil.
3. Repeat the process with several lengths of yarn, overlapping them to resemble a tangle of noodles. Allow time for the yarn to dry.
4. Glue the bowl to the red paper.
5. Remove the yarn from the aluminum foil and glue it above the bowl. Set the project aside to dry.

3-D George Washington

A little George Washington takes shape as a youngster completes this cute craft!

Supplies:

4½" cardboard tube
4½" x 6" white paper
2" x 6" black construction paper (jacket)
1" x 2" white construction paper (ruffle)
three 2" x 5½" black construction paper pieces (hat)

glue
marker
four cotton balls
decorative edge scissors
scissors

Setup:

Cut the 2" x 5½" black construction paper pieces into crescent shapes, as shown, for each child.

2 in.

←——— 5½ in. ———→

Steps:

1. Glue the larger white paper around the tube.
2. Glue the jacket around one end of the tube.
3. Use decorative edge scissors to trim each long side of the ruffle.
4. Glue the ruffle to the black strip.
5. Draw a face above the jacket.
6. Glue cotton balls to either side of the face and around the back of the tube. *(Glue three crescent cutouts at the points to make a three-cornered hat.)*
7. Place the hat atop the figure.

Beverly G. McCormick—Gr. K, East Brainerd Elementary School, Chattanooga, TN

Presidents' Day Crowns

Each youngster will love crafting this crowning reminder of presidents Abraham Lincoln and Thomas Jefferson!

Supplies:

3" x 24" red, white, or blue
   tagboard (headband)
tan paper
gray paper
large penny and nickel patterns (face side)

scissors
glue
red, blue, and silver
   star stickers
stapler

Setup:

Make a tan copy of the penny pattern and a gray copy of the nickel pattern.

Steps:

1. Cut out the paper coins.
2. Glue the cutouts to the center of a headband.
3. Attach star stickers. *(Size the headband to fit the child and then staple the ends together.)*

Betty Silkunas—Gr. K, Lower Gwynedd Elementary, Ambler, PA

Presidential Top Hat

Each student will be proud as a president when he wears his stovepipe hat fashioned like President Lincoln's.

Supplies:

two 12" x 18" black construction paper sheets
12" black construction paper circle (brim)
glue
pencil
scissors
stapler

Steps:

1. Glue together one 18-inch edge from each piece of black paper. Allow the glue to dry.
2. Make one-inch cuts along one long edge of the glued papers.
3. Fold up the resulting tabs. *(Form the paper into a tube and size it to fit the child's head. Staple the edges together.)*
4. Position the uncut end of the tube in the center of the brim. Trace around the tube.
5. Cut out the resulting circle in the center of the brim.
6. Glue the tabs to the brim to complete the hat.

Johanna Litts—Gr. K, North Central Elementary, Hermansville, MI

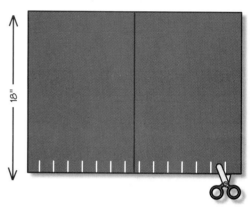

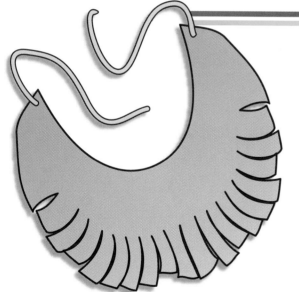

Abe's Brown Beard

There's no shaving required with this cute beard!

Supplies:

12" brown construction paper square
two 12" lengths of brown yarn
scissors
pencil
hole puncher
2 hole reinforcers

Setup:

Cut a beard shape from the brown paper.

Steps:

1. Make one-inch cuts along the edge of the beard.
2. Wrap the resulting paper tabs around a pencil to curl the beard.
3. Hole-punch each side of the beard.
4. Put a hole reinforcer around each hole.
5. Tie the end of a length of yarn to each hole. *(Size the beard to fit the child by tying the yarn ends together.)*

Johanna Litts—Gr. K

Happy Valentine's Day!

Marbleized Valentine

This uniquely decorated bag is perfect for youngsters' valentine cards or for a parent gift.

Supplies:

7" white construction paper heart
9" red construction paper heart
medium-size white paper bag
shallow box (slightly larger than the white heart)
red and pink tempera paints
2 marbles
2 spoons
glue
marker

Steps:

1. Lay the white heart in the box.
2. Dip one marble in pink paint and put it in the box.
3. Dip the other marble in red paint and put it in the box.
4. Tilt the box to roll the marbles across the cutout several times. Let the paint dry.
5. Glue the painted heart atop the red heart.
6. Glue the hearts onto the bag.
7. Write "Happy Valentine's Day!" on the bag.

Nancy Vogt—PreK, Boothbay Head Start, Boothbay, ME

Handy Heart Placemat

Show off youngsters' writing skills with this handy placemat.

Supplies:

12" x 18" red construction paper
white tempera paint
gold glitter glue
markers

My handy heart of gold!

Steps:

1. Apply paint to both hands.
2. Place hands in a heart position by touching the tips of the thumbs together and the tips of the index fingers together.
3. Make handprints on the red paper. Let the paint dry.
4. Outline the heart shape within the handprints with glitter glue. Let it dry.
5. Use a marker to draw a large heart shape around the handprints.
6. Write "My handy heart of gold!" at the bottom of the paper. *(Laminate the placemat.)*

adapted from an idea by Gail Marsh—Preschool and Pre-Kindergarten, St. Mark's Lutheran School, Eureka, MO

Cupid Cuties

What a fun holiday headband for all your little cupids!

Supplies:

two 3" x 9" pink construction paper strips (headband)
eight 2" red construction paper hearts
3" x 6" arrow (front half)
3" x 6" arrow (back half)
glue
stapler
scissors

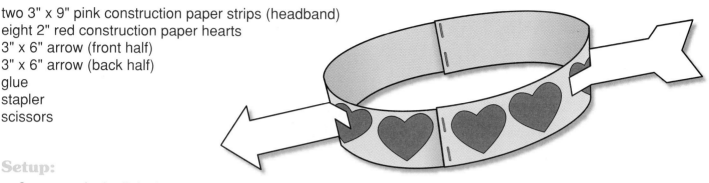

Setup:

Cut a one-inch slit in the middle of the straight end of each arrow half. Bend the resulting tabs in opposite directions as shown.

Steps:

1. Glue the hearts to the headband strips. Allow time for the glue to dry.
2. Glue the tabs on one arrow half in the middle of one headband strip; then repeat with the remaining arrow half and strip. Let the glue dry completely. *(Fit the two strips around the child's head and staple them together to make a headband.)*

Johanna Litts—Gr. K, North Central Elementary, Hermansville, MI

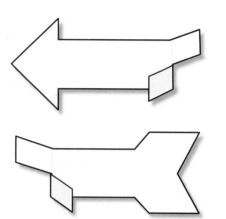

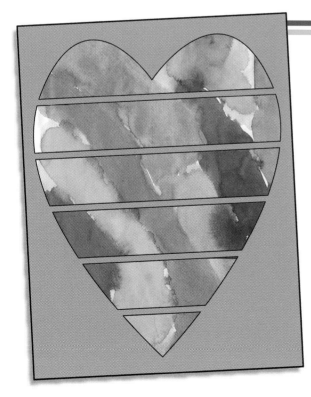

Broken Hearts

A set of these hearty watercolor paintings makes a beautiful Valentine's Day display.

Supplies:

8" white construction paper heart
8½" x 11" colored construction paper
watercolor paints
paintbrushes
scissors
glue

Steps:

1. Paint a design on the heart. Let the paint dry.
2. Cut the heart into several strips.
3. Glue the strips onto the colored paper, leaving a space between each strip, to re-create the heart shape.

Gail Marsh—Preschool and Pre-Kindergarten
St. Mark's Lutheran School, Eureka, MO

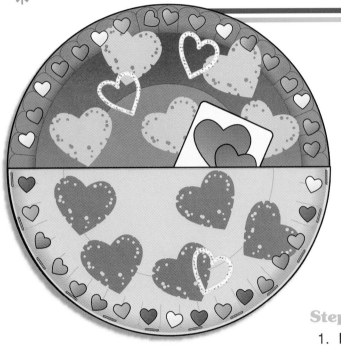

Valentine Card Caddy

Keep all those little love notes in this easy-to-make card holder.

Supplies:

paper plate
paper plate half
shallow dish of red tempera paint
shallow dish of pink tempera paint
paintbrush
heart-shaped sponge
heart-shaped sequins
glitter glue
stapler

Steps:

1. Paint the paper plate red. Let it dry. Sponge-paint several pink hearts. Set it aside to dry.
2. Paint the back of the half paper plate pink. Let it dry. Sponge-paint several red hearts. Let it dry.
3. Staple the two pieces together along the rim.
4. Decorate the holder with glitter glue and heart sequins.

Beth Allison—Preschool–Gr. 5 Art; Austinville, Benjamin Davis, and Frances Nungester Elementary Schools; Decatur, AL

Happy Heart Bouquet

Give a loved one a happy heart with this smiling gift bouquet.

Supplies:

two 3" construction paper hearts
2" construction paper heart
glue
small heart-shaped sequins
3 craft sticks
2" x 7" pink construction paper strip
marker

small heart stickers
3 oz. cup
small ball of clay
tape

Steps:

1. Glue sequins to each heart to form a face. Let the glue dry.
2. Glue each heart onto a separate craft stick.
3. Write "You Make My Heart Happy" on the paper strip and then decorate it with stickers.
4. Press the clay into the cup.
5. Tape the paper strip around the cup.
6. Push each craft stick into the clay.

Beth Allison—Preschool–Gr. 5 Art

Melted Valentine's Day Card

It's not melted chocolate but melted crayon shavings that give this valentine a unique design!

Supplies:

cheese grater
plastic bowl
old crayons with paper removed
9" x 12" white construction paper
newspaper
waxed paper
towel
iron (for teacher use only)
markers
8 ½" x 11" white copy paper
glue
4" construction paper heart
ribbon

Setup:

Place the grater in the bowl and grate a supply of crayon shavings.

Steps:

1. Place the white construction paper on top of the newspaper and then sprinkle on a handful of crayon shavings.
2. Place a sheet of waxed paper on top of the shavings.
3. Place the towel on top of the waxed paper. *(Use an iron on low setting to iron over the towel several times to melt the crayon shavings onto the paper. Let the paper cool.)*
4. Fold the paper with the design on the outside to make a card.
5. Write a valentine message on the white copy paper and decorate it as desired. Then glue it inside the card.
6. Accordion-fold the heart and glue it onto the front of the card.
7. Make a bow with the ribbon and glue it onto the heart. Let it dry.

Teresa Aten—Gr. K, Elm Creek Public School, Elm Creek, NE

Loving Picture

Self-expression shines through this loving work of art.

Supplies:

two 9" paper plates
scissors
small construction paper hearts
heart-shaped confetti
glue
markers
stapler

Setup:

Cut out and discard the center of one paper plate.

Steps:

1. Place the rim upside down. Glue paper hearts and confetti onto it, making a frame. Let it dry.
2. Draw a picture of something or someone you love in the center of the paper plate.
3. Place the frame on top of the picture. *(Staple the edges together.)*

Angie Kutzer—Gr. K, Garrett Elementary School, Mebane, NC

Sparkled Heart

A simple vegetable masher gives this heart creation a sparkling twist.

Supplies:

9" construction paper heart
vegetable masher
shallow dish of thinned glue
glitter
paper plate

Steps:

1. Dip the masher into glue and then stamp it repeatedly onto the heart.
2. Sprinkle on glitter. Let it dry.
3. Lift the heart and shake the excess glitter onto a paper plate.

Debbie Clark—Preschool, Preschool in the Park, Springfield, IL

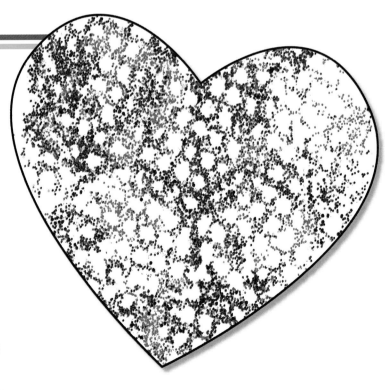

Spring

Flower Shadows

Templates are the key to making this bouquet of beautiful flowers!

Supplies:

tagboard flower templates in a variety of sizes
12" x 18" light-colored construction paper
shallow dishes of tempera paint
small sponges

Setup:

Place a sponge near each dish of paint.

Steps:

1. Place a template on the paper. Dip a sponge in the paint.
2. While holding the template in place, brush the sponge from the middle of the template outward onto the paper. Work around the entire flower in a similar fashion. Then remove the template.
3. Repeat the process, using different colors and templates. *(Encourage youngsters to overlap the flowers.)* Set the painting aside to dry.

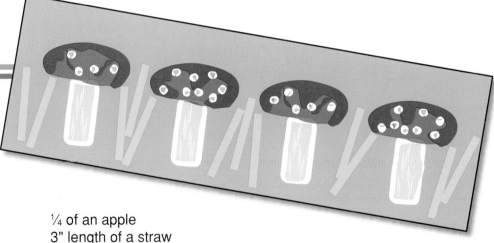

Mushrooms on the Lawn

This unique printmaking activity turns fungus into fun!

Supplies:

small rectangular block
shallow pans of white, red, and green tempera paint
6" x 18" blue construction paper

¼ of an apple
3" length of a straw
unsharpened pencil with eraser

Steps:

1. Dip the side of the block in the white paint. Make four prints on the paper to resemble mushroom stems.
2. Dip the apple in the red paint. Position the apple section horizontally and make a print above each rectangle to resemble the caps on mushrooms.
3. Dip the side of the straw in the green paint. Make prints around the mushrooms to resemble grass.
4. Dip the pencil eraser in the white paint. Print spots on each mushroom cap. Let it dry.

Pussy Willow Pictures

Youngsters use swirled black and white paint to make these pleasing pussy willows!

Supplies:

shallow pan
white and black tempera paint
plastic spoon

12" x 18" blue construction paper
brown marker
cotton ball

Setup:

Pour white paint in the pan. Add a small amount of black paint. Then swirl the colors together with the spoon so the paint has a streaked appearance.

Steps:

1. Use the brown marker to draw branches on the paper.
2. Dip the side of the cotton ball into the paint and then repeatedly press it along the branches, adding more paint to the cotton ball when necessary.
3. Set the picture aside to dry.

adapted from an idea by Deborah Garmon, Groton, CT

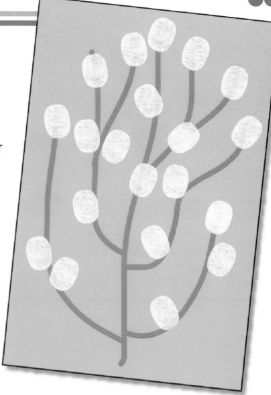

A Growing Garden

Little ones lend a hand in making this spring garden!

Supplies:

12" x 18" white construction paper
shallow pans of colorful tempera paint
green tempera paint
paintbrush

Steps:

1. Put your hand in a pan of paint; then make a handprint on the paper. Repeat.
2. Paint a stem and leaves below your print to resemble a flower.
3. Paint grass and insects around your flowers. Let the paint dry.

Teresa Howton—PreK, Kid's Kingdom on Broad, Scottsboro, AL

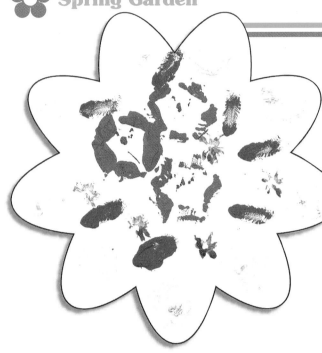

Posy Printing

Youngsters can thank Mother Nature for this fun print-making activity!

Supplies:

large white construction paper flower
several fresh flowers with stems
shallow pans of tempera paint

Steps:

1. Dip a fresh flower in the paint. Make prints on the paper.
2. Repeat the process with different flowers and colors of paint. Set the project aside to dry.

Dawn Rolita—Gr. K, World Cup Nursery School and Kindergarten, Chappaqua, NY

Spring Windsock

Little ones will be blown away by this flowery windsock!

Supplies:

12" x 18" light blue construction paper
green tempera paint
paintbrush
shallow pans of white, purple, and red tempera paint
glue
narrow strips of green crepe paper
green construction paper leaves
2" x 18" construction paper strip
stapler

Steps:

1. Paint grass and three stems on the paper.
2. Make a red handprint above a stem to resemble a tulip.
3. Make purple fingerprints above a stem to resemble a hyacinth.
4. Use your finger to paint white petals above the remaining stem to resemble a daisy. Allow time for the paint to dry.
5. Turn the paper over and glue crepe paper strips along the bottom edge.
6. Glue construction paper leaves to the crepe paper. Allow time for the glue to dry. *(Roll the paper into a cylinder and staple the edges together. Then staple the strip of construction paper to the top of the windsock to make a handle.)*

Dawn Rolita—Gr. K

Pretty As a Picture

This blooming frame is sure to make students smile! When the project is finished, encourage each youngster to take his frame home to place on the refrigerator.

Supplies:

7" x 8" craft foam
ruler
scissors
flat plastic flowers, such as those
    cut from a Hawaiian lei
glue
photograph of
    the child
self-adhesive
    magnetic strips

Setup:

For each child, cut a 3½" x 5" opening in the center of a piece of craft foam.

Steps:

1. Glue several flowers to the frame. Allow time for the glue to dry.
2. Place glue around the edges of the photo and glue it to the back of the frame so the photo shows through the opening. Set the project aside to dry.
3. Remove the adhesive backing from the magnetic strips. Attach them to the back of the frame.

Lynn C. Mode—Gr. K, Benton Heights Elementary, Monroe, NC

Fingerpaint Flowers

Youngsters make these bright and cheerful flowers from fingerpaintings!

Supplies:

2 sheets of 12" x 18" white fingerpaint paper
green fingerpaint
fingerpaint in a variety of floral colors
scissors
12" x 18" blue construction paper
glue

Steps:

1. Fingerpaint one sheet of the white paper green.
2. Fingerpaint the other sheet of white paper with two or three floral colors. Allow time for the paint to dry.
3. Cut stems, petals, and leaves from the paper and glue them to the blue paper to make a flower garden.

Lynn C. Mode—Gr. K

Painted Posies

Youngsters transform your classroom into a garden with colorful coffee filter flowers! Simply attach the finished posies to a bulletin board.

Supplies:

2 coffee filters
watercolor paints
paintbrush
glue

cupcake liner
green construction paper stem
green construction paper leaves

Steps:

1. Paint each coffee filter with watercolors. Allow time for the paint to dry.
2. Place a small amount of glue in the center of a coffee filter. Then stack the second filter on top.
3. Glue the cupcake liner to the center of the top filter. Allow time for the glue to dry.
4. Crumple and then shape the filters and liner to give the flower a realistic appearance.
5. Glue the flower to the top of the stem.
6. Glue leaves to the stem. Set the flower aside to dry.

Lisa Leonardi, Madison, CT

Walking in the Mud

With this cooperative project, youngsters can go walking through the mud without getting their feet dirty! Display the completed mural on a wall or bulletin board.

Supplies:

narrow length of white bulletin board paper
tape
large, shallow pan of brown paint
old pair of shoes
colorful construction paper
glue
scissors

Setup:

Tape the bulletin board paper to a table.

Steps:

1. Dip the bottoms of the shoes in the pan of paint. Then place a shoe on each hand and walk them across the paper. Allow time for the paint to dry.
2. Cut flowers and insects from construction paper and glue them to the mural.

adapted from ideas by Coramarie Marinan—Gr. K, Howe School, Green Bay, WI, and
Nancy M. Lotzer—Preschool, The Hillcrest Academy, Dallas, TX

Buzzin' Around

There will be quite a buzz about this artistic spring bulletin board!

Supplies:

narrow length of white bulletin board paper
tape
green marker
tempera paint in a variety of colors,
    including green and yellow
fine-tip black marker

Setup:

Place a length of bulletin board paper along a lower portion of your classroom wall. Add the title "What's the Buzz? It's Spring!"

Steps:

1. Use the green marker to draw several stems on the paper.
2. Make green fingerprints (leaves) on the stem.
3. Make colorful fingerprints (petals) above the stem.
4. Make yellow fingerprints (bees) around the flowers. Allow time for the paint to dry.
5. Use the black marker to add details to the bees, such as antennae, eyes, legs, wings, and stripes.

Pretty Pink Blossoms

Lovely cherry blossoms are popping out all over on this piece of artwork!

Supplies:

12" x 18" white construction paper
brown tempera paint
paintbrush
green tissue paper squares (leaves)
pink tissue paper squares (blossoms)
glue

Steps:

1. Paint a brown tree trunk and branches on the paper. Allow time for the paint to dry.
2. Crumple green tissue paper squares and glue them to the branches.
3. Crumple pink tissues paper squares and glue them to the branches.

69

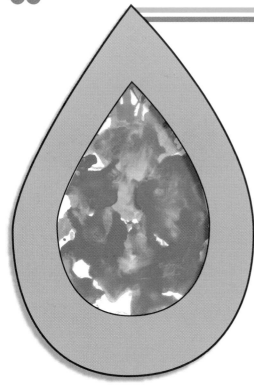

Puff Painting

The forecast for this drip-drop display is a puff of wind and a shower of fun!

Supplies:

scissors
9" x 12" blue construction paper
eyedroppers
thinned dark blue and
   light blue tempera paint
9" x 12" white construction paper
straw
glue

Setup:

Cut a large raindrop shape from the blue paper and then cut out the center to make a frame.

Steps:

1. Use an eyedropper to drip several drops of each paint onto the white paper.
2. Use the straw to blow the paint around the paper. Let it dry.
3. Glue the frame onto the painted paper.
4. Trim the excess paper away from the outside of the frame.

Jana Sanderson—Three- and Four-Year-Olds, Rainbow School, Stockton, CA

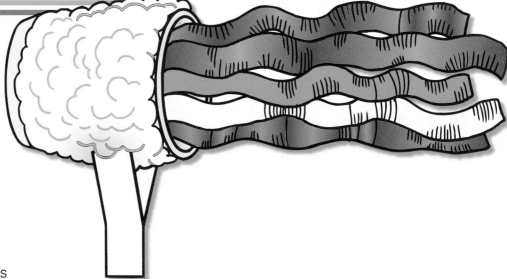

Windcatcher

Take this fun project outside to observe wind direction or use it indoors as a festive blower.

Supplies:

paper cup
scissors
1" x 8" posterboard strip
tape
cotton balls
glue
½" x 12" crepe paper streamers

Setup:

Cut a hole in the bottom of the cup to allow air to move through it.

Steps:

1. Fold the poster board strip in half; then fold back each end of the strip to make tabs. Tape the tabs onto the cup to make a handle.
2. Pull the cotton balls to stretch them into thinner pieces.
3. Spread glue all over the cup and then add cotton to resemble a cloud. Let it dry.
4. Tape the streamers to the inside bottom of the cup.
5. Take the windcatcher outside and hold it up by the handle to allow air to pass through it. Or blow air through the hole in the bottom of the cup to make the streamers flutter.

Rainbow Mobile

Brighten up a rainy day with a colorful display of rainbow mobiles!

Supplies:

paper plate
scissors
watercolor paints in rainbow colors
paintbrush

glue
clear cello shred
  (gift basket filler)
24" length of yarn

Setup:

Fold the paper plate in half and cut a semicircle from the folded edge as shown. Then unfold the plate.

Steps:

1. Lay the paper plate facedown and paint it in concentric circles, sequencing the colors like those in a rainbow. Let the paint dry.
2. Cut the plate along the fold line to make two rainbows. Spread glue on the unpainted side of each piece.
3. Press the cello shred onto the glue on one rainbow so that it will hang below it. Place the yarn on the glue at the top of the rainbow to use as a hanger.
4. Align the rainbows, glue sides facing, and press the two pieces together. Let it dry.

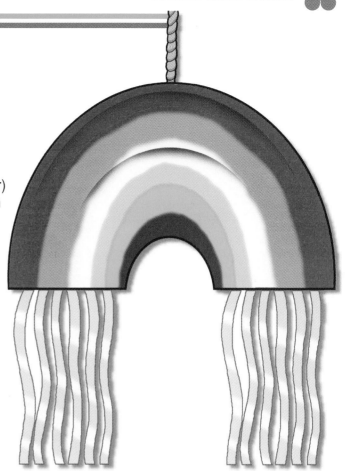

Wind Wand

Flutter through a windy day with this fun dancing wand.

Supplies:

thinned tempera paint
eyedropper
8½" x 11" white paper
straw

scissors
paper towel tube
glue
12" x ½" crepe paper strips

Steps:

1. Drip several different colors of paint onto the white paper.
2. Blow through the straw to streak the paint across the paper. Let it dry.
3. Trim the paper to fit the length and perimeter of the tube.
4. Wrap the paper around the tube and glue it in place.
5. Glue the crepe paper strips inside one end of the tube to make streamers.

Rainy Day Pops

This cool painting method adds interest to rainy day artwork.

Supplies:

food coloring   aluminum foil
water   craft sticks
ice cube tray   white paper

Setup:

Mix food coloring and water to make different paint colors. Then pour each color into a separate section of an ice cube tray. Cover the tray with aluminum foil. Then press a craft stick through the foil into each cube section. Freeze the colored water to make paint pops.

Steps:

1. Use the paint pops to paint a rainy day picture on the paper. Let it dry.
2. Display the paintings under the rain clouds from "Cloud Burst" below.

Coramarie Marinan—Gr. K, Howe School, Green Bay, WI

Cloud Burst

Watch for bursting clouds when this project is displayed together with "Rainy Day Pops" above!

Supplies:

coffee filter   eyedropper
7" aluminum foil square   paintbrush
blue watercolor paint   scissors
stapler

Steps:

1. Fold the filter in half.
2. Drip several drops of paint onto the filter. Let it dry.
3. Fold one edge of the foil several times.
4. Paint one side of the foil and let it dry.
5. Staple the folded edge of the foil onto the back of the filter at its fold.
6. Cut slits in the foil up to the filter to resemble rain.

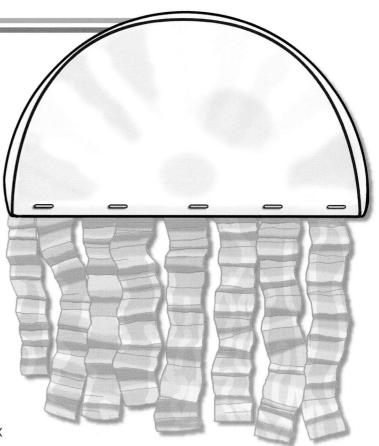

Nancy M. Lotzer—Preschool, The Hillcrest Academy, Dallas, TX

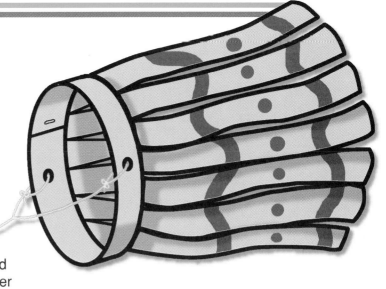

Cool Kite

This easy-to-make kite flutters on a windy day, and a group of them makes a cool classroom display.

Supplies:

18" x 24" bulletin board paper   scissors
18" x 2" poster board strip   hole puncher
stapler   heavy string
crayons

Setup:

Lay the paper vertically and lay the poster board strip along the top edge. Fold the top down to cover the poster board as shown. Staple the poster board in place.

Steps:

1. Color designs on the paper.
2. Cut the paper up to the folded section to make strips.
3. Roll the top section to make a cylinder and then staple it together.
4. Punch two holes at the top and tie on the string as shown.

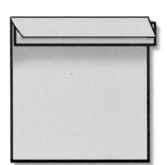

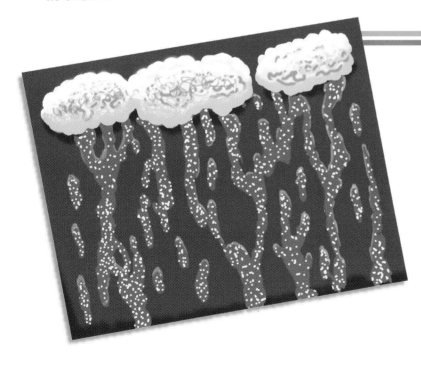

Drip-Drop Downpour

This shimmering rainstorm goes along with the study of spring clouds.

Supplies:

black construction paper   cotton balls
thinned glue   black marker
silver glitter   eyedropper

Steps:

1. Drip several drops of glue at the horizontal top of the paper.
2. Hold the paper up for several seconds to allow the glue to drip down the page.
3. Lay the paper on a flat surface and sprinkle it with glitter. Shake off the excess glitter.
4. Pull several cotton balls into cloud shapes and glue them to the top of the paper.
5. Use a marker to lightly color the cotton to make storm clouds.

Lisa Leonardi, Madison, CT

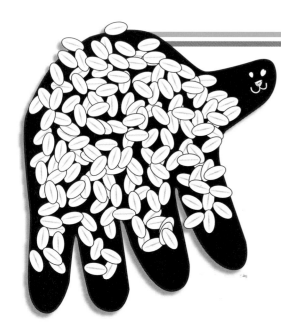

Woolly Little Lamb

A little oatmeal makes this little lamb's coat very realistic!

Supplies:

white or light-colored gel pen
4" x 6" piece of black construction paper
scissors
glue
dry oatmeal

Setup:

Trace a child's hand positioned with fingers slightly spread and the thumb pointed out. Cut out the handprint.

Steps:

1. Turn the cutout so the fingers face downward and draw a face on the tip of the thumb with the gel pen.
2. Without covering the fingers or thumb tip, spread a generous layer of glue onto the handprint.
3. Sprinkle oatmeal on the glue. Allow the glue to dry completely and then shake off the excess oatmeal.

Shondra Comeaux—Gr. K, Jolly Elementary, Clarkston, GA

"Hand-some" Lion

Evidence of a youngster's "hand-y" work makes this lion display "grrreat"!

Supplies:

brown tempera paint
paintbrush
12" yellow construction paper circle
scissors
construction paper scraps
glue
markers

Steps:

1. Paint the palm and fingers of one hand.
2. With fingers spread slightly and positioned toward the edge of the circle, press the painted hand onto the paper. Repeat the process all the way around the circle. Add more paint as needed.
3. Snip between the fingerprints to create a lion's mane.
4. Cut facial features from construction paper and glue them to the face. Add additional details with markers.

Nancy M. Lotzer—Preschool, The Hillcrest Academy, Dallas, TX

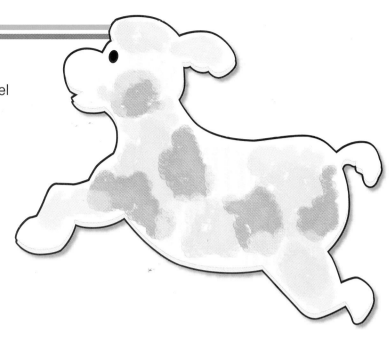

Lamb's Wool Painting

One little, two little, three little lambs! These pastel paintings make perfect fuzzy flannelboard counting sheep.

Supplies:

white felt lamb
pastel colored tempera paints
paintbrushes

Steps:

1. Paint the felt with assorted colors.
2. Experiment with mixing two different colors of paint together on the felt. Let the paint dry.

Coramarie Marinan—Gr. K, Howe School, Green Bay, WI

Calendar Critters

Use these calendar cover-ups as a visual check of the lion days and the lamb days!

Supplies:

3" yellow construction paper circle
3" white construction paper circle
yellow and brown tissue paper
3 cotton balls
black and tan construction paper scraps

scissors
glue
markers

Steps:

Lion:

1. Tear small pieces of each color of tissue paper. Glue a tissue paper mane around the edge of the yellow circle.
2. Cut ears from tan construction paper and glue them onto the lion.
3. Use markers to add facial features to the lion.

Lamb:

1. Stretch the cotton balls and glue them around the edge of the white circle.
2. Cut ears from black construction paper and glue them onto the lamb.
3. Use markers to add facial features to the lamb.

Frisky Lion

Rrrroar! Spring rushes in with this wild lion puppet.

Supplies:

5 coffee filters   scissors
stapler   construction paper scraps
brown watercolor paint   glue
paintbrush   markers

Setup:

Stack the filters one on top of the next. Then staple them together around the inner circle, leaving an open space large enough for several fingers to fit.

Steps:

1. Paint both sides of the stack of filters. Let the paint dry.
2. Cut from the outer edge of the stack of filters to the inner circle of the filters several times to create a lion mane.
3. Fluff the edges of the mane.
4. Place the opening at the bottom; then cut construction paper facial features and glue them on. Add additional details with markers.
5. Place fingers in the opening to use the puppet.

Nancy M. Lotzer—Preschool, The Hillcrest Academy, Dallas, TX

Lopsy Lamb

Baa, baa. Greet spring with this quiet little lamb puppet.

Supplies:

5 coffee filters   construction paper scraps
stapler   glue
scissors   markers

Setup:

Stack the filters one on top of the next. Then staple them together around the inner circle, leaving an open space large enough for several fingers to fit.

Steps:

1. Cut from the outer edge to the inner circle of the filters several times to create lamb's wool.
2. Fluff the edges.
3. Place the opening at the bottom; then cut construction paper facial features and glue them on. Add additional details with markers.
4. Place fingers in the opening to use the puppet.

Nancy Lotzer—Preschool

Double Duty

March in as a lion and march out like a lamb with this double-sided headband!

Supplies:

white paper plate
scissors
ruler
crayons
4 dot stickers (eyes)
4 hole reinforcers (eyes)
yellow, brown, and orange yarn (lion's mane)
black and brown construction paper scraps
cotton balls
glue
2" x 18" poster board headband
stapler

Setup:

Cut yarn into two-inch pieces. Cut the paper plate in half.

Steps:

Lion:

1. Color one plate half yellow. Position the plate so that the straight side is the bottom.
2. Make each eye by sticking a hole reinforcer on top of a dot sticker. Stick two on the plate half.
3. Draw and color a nose and mouth.
4. Cut ears from brown paper and glue them on the plate.
5. Glue a yarn mane around the face. Let it dry.

Lamb:

1. Position the other plate half so that the straight side is the bottom.
2. Make two eyes, as described in Step 2 above, and stick them to the plate half.
3. Draw and color a nose and mouth near the cut edge.
4. Cut ears from black paper and glue them on the plate.
5. Stretch out several cotton balls and glue them around the face. Let it dry. *(Size the headband to the child's head and staple the ends together. Position the lion on one side of the headband and staple it in place. Position the lamb on the other side of the headband and staple it in place.)*

Jana Sanderson—Three- and Four-Year-Olds, Rainbow School, Stockton, CA

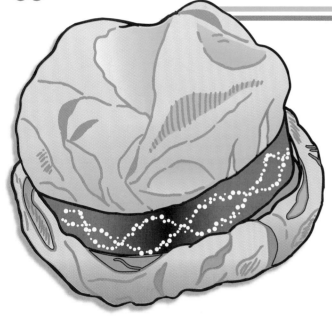

Lucky Leprechaun Hat

No one will catch your little ones without their green when they wear these lucky hats!

Supplies:

large brown paper bag
masking tape
green tempera paint
paintbrush

1 yard length of black
  crepe paper
gold glitter
glue
stapler

Setup:

Turn the bag inside out and position it so the opening is at the bottom. Roll up the edges to create a hat with a brim. Wrap masking tape around the base of the hat above the brim.

Steps:

1. Paint the hat green and set it aside to dry.
2. To create a hatband, squeeze glue in a random design along the crepe paper. Then sprinkle glitter on the glue. Let the glue dry.
3. Shake off the excess glitter; then wrap the band around the hat, trim as needed, and staple the ends together.

Jana Sanderson—Three- and Four-Year-Olds, Rainbow School, Stockton, CA

Leprechaun Footprints

Leaping leprechauns! Invite youngsters to follow a trail of leprechaun footprints to find a pot of special treats!

Supplies:

36" strip of adding machine tape
shallow pan of green tempera paint
tape

Setup:

Tape the adding machine strip along the edge of a table.

Steps:

1. Make a fist and carefully dip the pinky side into the paint. Starting at one end of the paper strip, press your paint-covered fist onto the paper. Continue in this manner, alternating hands, until the strip has several prints.
2. Dip a fingertip into the paint; then repeatedly press finger prints onto the end of each fist print to resemble toes. Let the paint dry. Tape each strip of footprints together to form a trail.

Nancy M. Lotzer—Preschool, The Hillcrest Academy, Dallas, TX

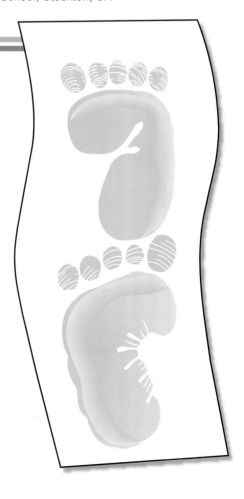

Lucky Play Dough

Invite a lucky little leprechaun to use this glittery dough to create a lucky pot of gold!

Supplies:

2 c. flour
1 c. salt
1 tsp. cream of tartar
2 c. water
yellow food coloring
yellow glitter
green glitter
pot
spoon
access to stove
　(teacher use)
chocolate coins wrapped
　in gold foil (optional)

Setup:

To prepare play dough, mix the first seven supplies together. Cook over medium heat, stirring continuously, until the mixture appears dry. Remove the mixture from the pan and cool. Store in an airtight container. (The recipe will make about five pots.)

Steps:

1. Roll a handful of dough into a smooth ball.
2. Shape the ball into a pot shape.
3. Pinch around the edges to form a smooth rim. Dry the resulting pot in an oven at 150°. Set it aside to cool.
4. If desired, fill the pot with chocolate coins.

Nancy M. Lotzer—Preschool, The Hillcrest Academy, Dallas, TX

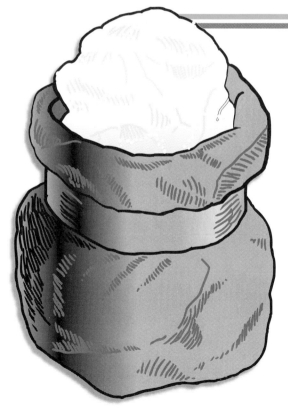

Pot of Gold

With a wee bit of paint and a sprinkling of glitter, your youngsters can make these festive pots of gold.

Supplies:

brown paper lunch bag
masking tape
newspaper
black tempera paint
paintbrush
glue
yellow tissue paper
gold glitter

Setup:

Roll down the edge of the paper bag to create the rim of a pot. Wrap tape around the bag below the roll to create a pot shape.

Steps:

1. Crumple newspaper and stuff it into the pot to create a dome above the rim.
2. Paint the pot black and allow the paint to dry.
3. Squeeze glue onto the tissue paper in a random design. Sprinkle glitter on the glue. When the glue is dry, shake off the excess glitter.
4. Tuck the tissue paper into the pot glitter-side out.

Jana Sanderson—Three- and Four-Year-Olds, Rainbow School, Stockton, CA

A Spot of Irish Tea Art

If you were to visit Ireland, you would find that teatime comes around three times a day! After sharing this information, invite your youngsters to use tea as a painting medium. Then display the paintings with a large colorful teapot cutout on a bulletin board titled "A Spot of Irish Tea Art."

Supplies:

black tea in bags
water
paintbrush
white paper

Setup:

Place the tea bags in a bowl of water. Allow the tea to steep for five to ten minutes, until the water turns a brownish color.

Step:

Dip the paintbrush into the tea and then paint a desired picture onto the paper. Let it dry. *(Cut out a shamrock shape from the paper.)*

Coramarie Marinan—Gr. K, Howe School, Green Bay, WI

Shamrock Showcase

Engage in some color mixing with this stunning shamrock project!

Supplies:

yellow and blue tempera paints
paintbrushes
3 white heart-shaped doilies
glue
black construction paper
green construction paper stem

Steps:

1. Paint each doily yellow. While the doily is still wet, paint over it again with blue paint. Let the paint dry.
2. Glue the doilies onto the black paper to form a shamrock.
3. Add a green construction paper stem.

Mary Lou Rodriguez—Gr. K, Primary Plus Elementary School, San Jose, CA

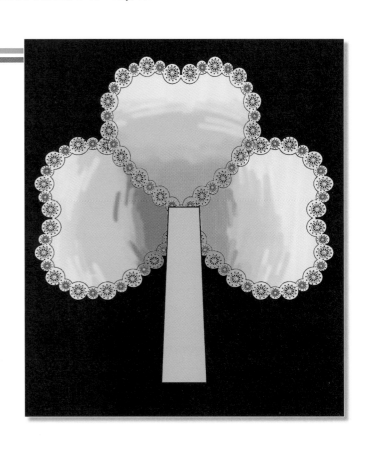

Shimmery Window Art

These shamrocks are sure to dazzle everyone who catches a glimpse of them.

Supplies:

laminating film or transparency sheet
dish soap
blue and yellow fingerpaint
scissors
clear tape

Steps:

1. Squirt one teaspoon of dish soap onto the laminating film.
2. Use your fingers to spread the soap over the film. (The soap will help the paint stick.)
3. Place a dab of blue and a dab of yellow fingerpaint atop the film. Use your fingers to blend the colors together and cover the film. Let the paint dry. *(Cut out a shamrock from the film.)*
4. Tape the shamrock to a window.

Coramarie Marinan—Gr. K, Howe School, Green Bay, WI

Shades of Green

Showcase the colors of this special day with this festive shamrock.

Supplies:

white paper
green, black, and white tempera paints
scissors
black marker (optional)

Setup:

Have students observe as you make dark green paint by mixing green paint and black paint in a shallow pan. Make light green paint by mixing white paint and green paint in another pan. Also set out a pan of green paint.

Steps:

1. Dip your finger into a paint pan and then onto the paper. In turn, dip your finger into the other two colors and then onto the paper, creating additional lighter and darker shades. Continue in this manner until the paper is painted. Allow the paint to dry. *(Cut the paper into a shamrock shape.)*
2. If desired, add a St. Patrick's Day message.

Coramarie Marinan—Gr. K

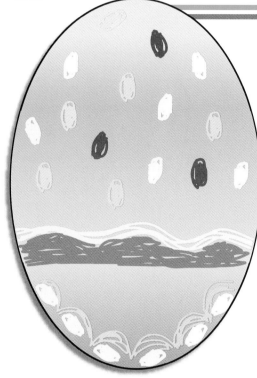

Colorful Egg Art

There's no need to worry about this egg breaking. It's made from paper, crayons, and paint!

Supplies:

white construction paper egg
crayons
pastel-colored water-thinned paint

paintbrush
book (or other heavy object)

Steps:

1. Use crayons to draw designs on the egg.
2. Paint the entire egg. Allow the paint to dry.
3. Place a heavy book on the cutout overnight to flatten the paper.

Teresa Aten—Gr. K, Elm Creek Public School, Elm Creek, NE

Hidden Eggs

Students can go on an egg hunt after they complete this cute craft! Post the projects side by side on a bulletin board to make an attractive egg hunt display.

Supplies:

white construction paper eggs
watercolor paints
paintbrush
glitter glue
crayons
9" x 12" light blue
   construction paper

3" x 12" green
   construction
   paper strip
stapler
scissors
glue

Steps:

1. Paint the eggs as desired. Let the paint dry.
2. Add glitter glue to the eggs. Allow the glue to dry.
3. Fold up two inches of one long side of the blue paper and staple the ends to make a pocket.
4. Make one-inch fringe cuts along one long edge of the green paper strip.
5. Glue the strip to the pocket.
6. Draw clouds and a sun.
7. Hide the eggs in the grassy pocket.

Lenny D. Grozier, Binghamton, NY

Tie-Dyed Egg

Try this twist on dying an egg, which uses markers, water, and a coffee filter! Save the pretty coffee filter to make the butterfly project below.

Supplies:

coffee filter
bright, washable markers
boiled egg

clothespin
spray bottle of water

Steps:

1. Color the entire coffee filter with various colors.
2. Place the egg in the center of the filter.
3. Gather the filter around the egg and clip the edges with the clothespin.
4. Spritz the filter with water. Allow it to dry.
5. Remove the clothespin and unwrap the egg.

Note: Do not allow the egg to be eaten.

Teresa Aten—Gr. K, Elm Creek Public School, Elm Creek, NE

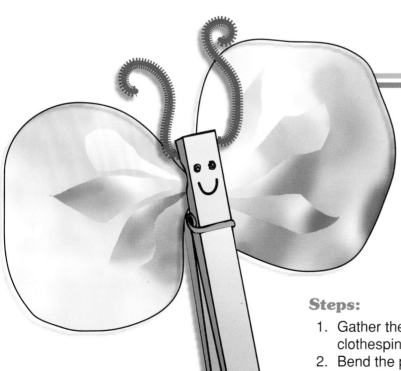

Coffee Filter Butterfly

The coffee filter from "Tie-Dyed Egg" (above) is put to good use when a youngster uses it to make this colorful butterfly.

Supplies:

colorful coffee filter
  (from the idea above)
clothespin

pipe cleaner half
fine-tip marker

Steps:

1. Gather the coffee filter in the center and clip it with the clothespin.
2. Bend the pipe cleaner piece and clip it with the clothespin.
3. Draw a face to complete the butterfly.

Teresa Aten—Gr. K

 **Easter**

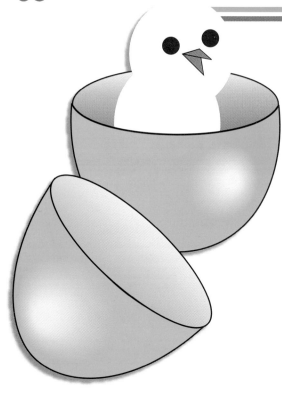

Hatching Baby Chick

This cute chick hatches again and again!

Supplies:

hole puncher
black construction paper scrap
orange construction paper scrap
scissors

glue
2 yellow cotton balls
plastic Easter egg

Setup:

Hole-punch the black paper to make two eyes. Fold the orange paper. Along the fold, cut a triangle-shaped beak.

Steps:

1. Glue one cotton ball in the bottom of the egg.
2. Glue the other cotton ball on top of the first one.
3. Glue on the eyes and beak. Let the glue dry.
4. Snap on the top of the egg.

Beverly McCormick—Gr. K, East Brainerd Elementary School, Chattanooga, TN

Bright Baskets

Recycled soda bottles provide the bases for these colorful baskets.

Supplies:

clean two-liter soda bottle
scissors
masking tape
assorted tissue paper squares
thinned glue

paintbrush
stapler
shredded paper (optional)
plastic eggs (optional)

Setup:

Cut a two-liter soda bottle in half and set aside the bottom portion to use as the basket. Cut a one-inch strip from the top half of the bottle to form a handle. Discard the remaining bottle top scraps. Cover the cut edges of the bottle bottom and handle with masking tape.

Steps:

1. Brush thinned glue on an outside area of the basket.
2. Cover the wet glue with overlapping tissue paper squares.
3. Repeat Steps 1 and 2 until the outside of the basket is covered. Turn it upside down and set it aside to dry.
4. Brush thinned glue on the top of the handle. Cover it with tissue paper squares. Allow the glue to dry.
5. Staple the handle to the basket. If desired, fill the basket with shredded paper and plastic eggs for Easter.

Dana Wiggins—4K, Latta Elementary School, Latta, SC

"Hop-py" Easter Art

Hop on down the bunny trail for some hippity-hoppity painting fun! Use the resulting painted paper to make decorative egg, flower, or basket cutouts.

Supplies:

large plastic peanut butter jar
white construction paper
scissors
small plastic eggs (one for
    each color of paint)

tape
cups of tempera paints
plastic spoons (one for
    each color of paint)

Setup:

Cut the paper to fit the inside of the jar. Tape the plastic eggs closed.

Steps:

1. Line the inside of the jar with a paper strip.
2. Drop an egg in each cup of paint.
3. Spoon a paint-covered egg into the jar and secure the lid.
4. Hold the jar on its side and hop.
5. Change eggs and hop again.
6. Allow the paint to dry. Remove the paper from the jar.

Jana Sanderson—Three- and Four-Year-Olds, Rainbow School, Stockton, CA

"Hand-some" Hare

The result of this handy painting technique is a super cute bunny that is unique to each child!

Supplies:

9" x 12" bright pink
    construction paper
white tempera paint
paintbrush
child's old sneaker

2 black pom-poms (eyes)
pink pom-pom (nose)
cotton ball (tail)
glue
crayons

Setup:

Paint the palm of a child's hand and first two fingers. Press his hand on the pink paper to make a bunny head.

Steps:

1. Paint the sole of the shoe. Press it on the paper to make a bunny body behind the head. Allow the paint to dry.
2. Glue the eyes and nose to the face.
3. Glue on the tail. Allow the glue to dry.
4. Use crayons to draw a mouth and whiskers. Draw grass and sky, if desired.

Lisa Leonardi, Madison, CT

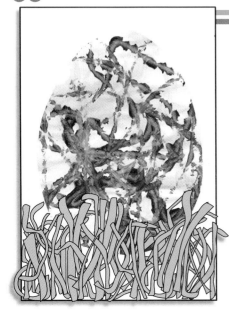

Eye-Catching Egg

The roll of a hard-boiled egg makes this Easter masterpiece!

Supplies:

9" x 12" white construction
  paper egg
shirt box with lid
tempera paint in various colors
hard-boiled egg for each container
  of paint
plastic spoons
glue
12" x 18" yellow construction
  paper
shredded green tissue
  paper

Setup:

Place a hard-boiled egg into each color of paint.

Steps:

1. Put the egg cutout in the box.
2. Spoon one paint-covered egg on top of the paper egg. Put the lid on the box.
3. Tilt the box to roll the egg over the cutout.
4. Remove the egg and return it to its paint container. Repeat Steps 2 and 3 with different colors of paint. Allow the paint to dry.
5. Glue the paper egg onto the yellow paper.
6. Glue the shredded tissue below the egg.

Lisa Leonardi, Madison, CT

Foil-Covered Chocolate

This egg looks and smells good enough to eat. Too bad it's only paper!

Supplies:

9" x 12" white construction
  paper egg
brown tempera paint
paintbrush
unsweetened cocoa powder
12" x 18" aluminum foil piece
permanent markers

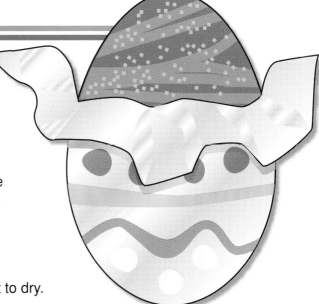

Steps:

1. Paint the egg cutout brown.
2. Sprinkle the wet paint with powdered cocoa. Allow the paint to dry.
3. Decorate the foil with markers.
4. Partially cover the chocolate egg with the decorative foil wrapper.

Jana Sanderson—Three- and Four-Year-Olds, Rainbow School, Stockton, CA

Stained Glass Look-Alike

This egg decoration lights up a window just like stained glass. Beautiful!

Supplies:

8½" x 11" transparency-film egg   tempera paint in various colors
white glue   paintbrush

Setup:

Mix glue and paint to make colored glue.

Step:

Paint the cutout with different colors of glue. Allow the glue to dry.

Coramarie Marinan—Gr. K, Howe School, Green Bay, WI

Jelly Bean Stamps

Reinforce colors, counting, or just creativity with these original stamps.

Supplies:

large jelly bean   2 film canisters
knife (for teacher use)   shallow dishes of tempera paint
hot glue (for teacher use)   white construction paper jelly bean

Setup:

Cut the jelly bean in half lengthwise. Hot-glue each half to the bottom of a separate film canister so that the jelly bean's flat side can be used for printing.

Steps:

1. Dip a jelly bean stamp in the paint and press prints onto the paper jelly bean.
2. Repeat using a different stamp and a different color of paint. *(If desired, have students stamp and count a predetermined number or color of jelly beans.)*

Mom's Nifty Notebook

This picture-perfect notebook is just right for Mom's purse. She simply adds phone numbers, lists, or reminders. How practical!

Supplies:

two 4" x 6" clear Con-Tact
   paper rectangles
child's photograph
2" colored tissue paper
   squares

scissors
8 or more 3" x 4" sheets
   of white paper
stapler
4" length of electrical tape

Setup:

Peel the backing off of one sheet of Con-Tact paper. Place the paper sticky side up on a table.

Steps:

1. Put the photograph facedown in the middle of the left half of the Con-Tact paper.
2. Place tissue paper squares on the Con-Tact paper to cover it. *(Peel the backing off of the other sheet of Con-Tact paper and carefully align it on top of the tissue-covered Con-Tact paper. Trim extra tissue paper that extends beyond the edges.)*
3. Fold the Con-Tact paper in half to make the booklet cover.
4. Insert the white paper and staple along the side.
5. Cover the staples with electrical tape.

adapted from an idea by Mary Lou Rodriguez—Gr. K, Primary Plus Elementary School, San Jose, CA

Carry Me Key!

This cute key chain is easy for Mom to pick up and carry everywhere!

Supplies:

small plastic lid (with no text)
hole puncher
craft foam in a variety of skin tones
scissors
permanent marker

fabric ribbon
key ring
glue
crayons
yarn in a variety of hair colors

Setup:

Punch a hole near the edge of the lid. Cut a circle from the craft foam to fit inside the lid.

Steps:

1. Use a marker to write a personal message on the top of the lid.
2. Thread the ribbon through the hole. Pull so the ends are equal and knot onto the lid. *(Knot the remaining ends to the key ring.)*
3. Glue the foam circle inside the lid.
4. With the ribbon positioned at the top, draw a face on the foam.
5. Cut yarn to match your hair and glue it onto the foam. Let it dry.

Jana Sanderson—Three- and Four-Year-Olds, Rainbow School, Stockton, CA

Momma Bird's House

A little bird said that this is a "tweet" gift! Customize the number of baby birds perched in this birdhouse to match the number of children in each child's family.

Supplies:

clean pint-size milk carton (birdhouse)
4" x 12" piece of colorful construction paper
glue
scissors
X-acto knife (teacher use only)
eight ¾" x 3" brown construction paper strips (shingles)
2" square of white paper

marker
Spanish moss
large red pom-pom (mother bird)
small yellow pom-poms (baby birds)
wiggle-eye stickers (2 per bird)
3 small craft feathers
scrap-paper beaks (1 per bird)

Setup:

Glue the paper rectangle around the sides of the milk carton to cover it; trim any excess paper. When the glue is dry, use the X-acto knife to cut a two-inch square in one side of the carton.

Steps:

1. Glue the shingles to the top of the birdhouse. Let the glue dry.
2. Personalize a message for Mom on the white paper and then glue it to one side of the birdhouse.
3. Make a nest of Spanish moss inside the birdhouse.
4. Stick wiggle-eye stickers on the large pom-pom. Then glue on a beak and three tail feathers. Let the glue dry.
5. For each baby bird, glue a beak to a small pom-pom and stick on wiggle-eye stickers. Let the glue dry.
6. Glue the mother bird just outside the opening to the birdhouse.
7. Put each of the baby birds inside the birdhouse.

adapted from an idea by Teri Burch—Gr. K,
Fernan, Coeur d'Alene, ID

Petite Potpourri Gift

Deliver this aromatic gift with a sweet Mother's Day song!

Supplies:

glue	1" colored tissue paper
water	squares
paintbrush	copy of the song below
clean, small plastic spice jar	plain index card
potpourri	crayons

Setup:

Mix together three parts glue and one part water.

Steps:

1. Remove the jar lid and brush the glue mixture onto a small area of the jar.
2. Put several tissue paper squares on the glue.
3. Repeat Steps 1 and 2 until the jar is completely covered.
4. Careful apply another layer of solution over the entire jar. Let it dry.
5. Fill the jar with potpourri and replace the lid.
6. Glue the copy of the song onto the card.
7. Personalize and decorate the card as desired.
8. Present the gift and card to Mom and sing the song to her.

Lenny D. Grozier, Binghamton, NY

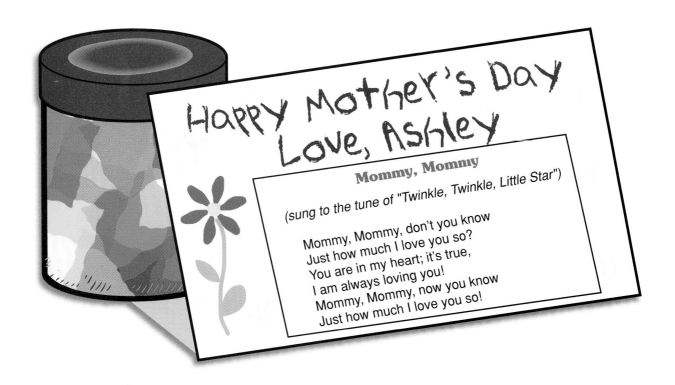

Happy Mother's Day
Love, Ashley

Mommy, Mommy

(sung to the tune of "Twinkle, Twinkle, Little Star")

Mommy, Mommy, don't you know
Just how much I love you so?
You are in my heart; it's true,
I am always loving you!
Mommy, Mommy, now you know
Just how much I love you so!

Veggie Vase

Various veggie prints create this unique bouquet of flowers!

Supplies:

9" x 12" sheet of colored construction paper
9" x 12" sheet of white construction paper
shallow dishes of tempera paint
green bell pepper half
potato half

carrot half
scissors
markers
glue

Setup:

Draw a vase shape onto the colored construction paper.

Steps:

1. Dip a potato or pepper in paint and press it onto the white paper. Repeat using each of those vegetables several times; keep the prints close together.
2. Dip the carrot half into a different color of paint and press it in the center of each flower print. Let the paint dry. *(Cut around the group of prints to make a flower bouquet.)*
3. Cut out the vase and write a personal message on it.
4. Glue the bouquet onto the top of the vase.

Ada Goren, Winston-Salem, NC

Very Important Mom

Mom will appreciate this useful, personalized business card holder.

Supplies:

2½" x 4" tagboard (card)
markers

plastic cassette case
stickers

Setup:

Write "Happy Mother's Day" on the tagboard.

Steps:

1. Open the case and lay it flat on the table, outside facing up.
2. Put stickers all over the surface of the case.
3. Use markers to decorate and personalize the card; then place it in the case.

Mary Lou Rodriguez—Gr. K, Primary Plus Elementary School, San Jose, CA

Fiesta Ring

Swirl, twist, and dance with this fun craft, which is ready for a party!

Supplies:

7" tagboard circle
scissors
12" crepe paper streamers in bright colors
cotton swabs
tempera paints
glue

Setup:

Cut a three-inch circle from the middle of the tagboard circle. Cut the streamers into thin strips.

Steps:

1. Use cotton swabs to dot paint on one side of the ring. Let it dry.
2. Turn the ring over and glue streamers around the edges.

Lynn C. Mode—Gr. K, Benton Heights Elementary, Monroe, NC

Party Maracas

Enhance the dance festivities mentioned in the activity above by adding these simple shakers. Cha-cha-cha!

Supplies:

two 16 oz. soda bottles (labels removed)
small colorful beads (for teacher use)
hot glue gun (for teacher use)
several 16" strands curling ribbon in bright colors
bright-colored permanent markers

Setup:

Put several beads in each bottle. Use hot glue to secure the lid on each bottle.

Steps:

1. Tie several strands of curling ribbon around the neck of each bottle.
2. Decorate each bottle using the markers.

Mini Piñata

This tiny treat holder is just right for a little one's Cinco de Mayo celebration.

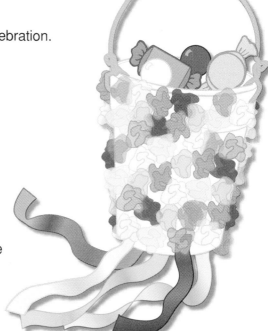

Supplies:

bright-colored 4" crepe paper
  streamers
scissors
foam cup
glue
paintbrush

pencil
bright-colored 3" tissue
  paper squares
pipe cleaner
wrapped candy and/or
  stickers

Setup:

Cut the streamers into thin strips. Demonstrate how to twist a tissue paper square around the eraser end of the pencil and glue the tissue paper to a cup.

Steps:

1. Set the cup upside down on a flat surface.
2. Brush glue onto a section of the cup.
3. Twist a tissue paper square around the eraser end of the pencil and press it onto the glue. Let it set for a few moments, remove the pencil, and then repeat until the glue is covered.
4. Repeat Steps 2 and 3 until much of the cup is covered.
5. Glue several streamers onto the cup's bottom. Let the glue dry.
6. Turn the cup right side up and poke the ends of the pipe cleaner through the rim to form a handle. Twist the ends to secure.
7. Fill the piñata with the treats.

Mary Lou Rodriguez—Gr. K, Primary Plus Elementary School, San Jose, CA

Pretty Pottery

Unique designs make this pottery look-alike fun to display museum-style.

Supplies:

orange and brown tempera paint
pictures of pottery (optional)
foam cup
masking tape

paintbrush
oil pastel crayons
hairspray

Setup:

Mix orange and brown paint to form a terra-cotta shade. If desired, show youngsters pictures of different pottery designs.

Steps:

1. Tear one-inch pieces of masking tape and apply them to the cup. Continue applying the tape, slightly overlapping it, until the cup is covered (including the bottom).
2. Paint the cup with the paint mixture. Set it aside to dry.
3. The next day, use oil pastels to draw colorful designs on the cup. *(Spray the finished design with hairspray to protect it.)*

Mary Lou Rodriguez—Gr. K

Festive Food

Create a display that will make passersby look twice. This texture-rich Mexican meal looks real!

Supplies:

1 tbsp. rubbing alcohol
yellow food coloring
2 c. dry rice
large resealable plastic bag
newspaper
glue
5" tan construction paper circle (tortilla)
yellow tissue paper strips (cheese)

rolled bits of brown tissue paper
  (beans)
paper plate
empty thread spool
shallow dish of red tempera paint
cotton balls
green-tinted glue
green tissue paper strips (guacamole)

Setup:

Make colored rice by placing the first three supplies in the plastic bag. Mix well and then spread the rice onto newspaper. Allow it to dry completely.

Steps:

1. Glue cheese onto the tortilla.
2. Glue beans atop the cheese.
3. To form a burrito, roll the tortilla and glue the edges where they meet.
4. Glue the burrito to the plate.
5. Dip the spool in red paint and press it onto the plate several times to form tomato slices.
6. Stretch a cotton ball and glue it to the plate for sour cream.
7. Squirt a puddle of glue on the plate and cover it with colored rice.
8. Squirt a small puddle of tinted glue on the plate and place the green tissue paper shreds in it for guacamole.

Lisa Leonardi, Madison, CT

 # Summer

Sunny Jellyfish

Turn a plain window into a splendid underwater display when you add this jellyfish suncatcher.

Supplies:

two 10" clear Con-Tact paper squares	black permanent marker
1" tissue paper squares	tissue paper strips
scissors	tape

Setup:

Remove the backing from one square of Con-Tact paper. Place it sticky side up on a tabletop.

Steps:

1. Press tissue paper squares onto the Con-Tact paper. *(Remove the backing from the remaining square of Con-Tact paper and place it on the decorated square. Then cut a semicircle from the Con-Tact paper.)*
2. Use the marker to draw a face.
3. Flip the jellyfish over. Tape the strips to the bottom edge.

Deborah Ryan—Preschool, Early Head Start Family Center of Portland
Portland, OR

Mr. Snappy

This cute little turtle is sure to make a splash with your little ones.

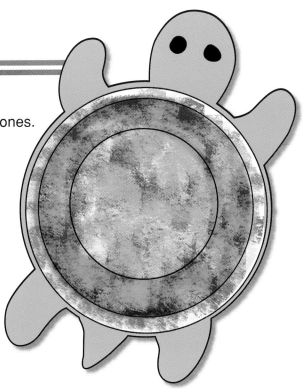

Supplies:

disposable paper bowl
green, yellow, and blue tempera paint
small sponges
glue
green construction paper turtle, slightly larger than the bowl
black marker

Steps:

1. Sponge-paint the bottom of the bowl yellow, blue, and green. Allow time for the paint to dry.
2. Place glue around the inside rim of the bowl.
3. Press the bowl onto the turtle.
4. Use the marker to draw eyes on the turtle. Set the project aside to dry.

Deborah Ryan—Preschool

Sticky Feet

What has eight tentacles, a green body, and a great big grin? This nifty octopus!

Supplies:

green construction paper octopus body
8 green construction paper strips
glue
suction cup with hanger
shallow dish of white tempera paint
black marker

Steps:

1. Glue each strip to the bottom edge of the body.
2. Flip the body over. Press the suction cup into the white paint. Make several prints along each strip, adding more paint to the suction cup when necessary.
3. Make two prints on the body to resemble eyes. Allow time for the paint to dry.
4. Use the black marker to draw pupils and a mouth.

Heather Lynn Miller—PreK, Creative Playschool, Auburn, IN

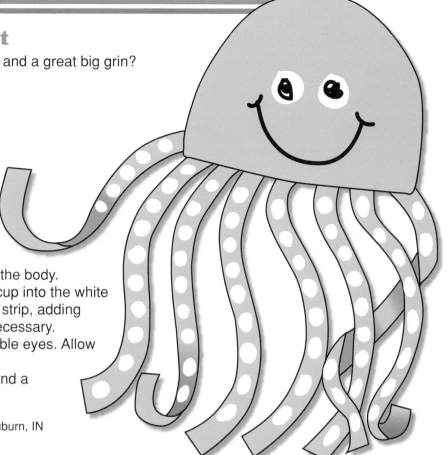

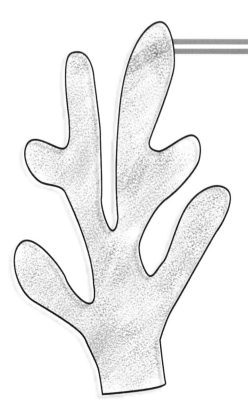

Colorful Coral

Dazzle your little ones with this easy-to-prepare coral craft.

Supplies:

copy paper
colorful pastels or chalk
plastic canvas
hairspray (for teacher use)
scissors

Steps:

1. Place the canvas under a sheet of copy paper.
2. Color over the paper with the pastels or chalk. *(Spray the project with hairspray to prevent smearing. Then cut a coral shape from the paper.)*

Lynn C. Mode—Gr. K, Benton Heights Elementary, Monroe, NC

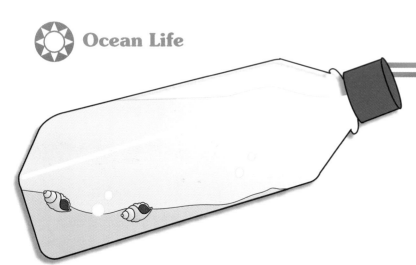

An Ocean of My Own

The result of this craft is a mini ocean that's sure to enthrall young and old alike!

Supplies:

small see-through plastic bottle with cap
sand
water
blue food coloring
tablespoon
bubble solution
electrical tape
small seashells (optional)

Steps:

1. Pour a small amount of sand in the bottle.
2. Partially fill the bottle with water.
3. Add drops of food coloring.
4. Add two tablespoons of bubble solution. *(If desired, drop in a few small shells. Tightly screw on the cap. Tape the cap to the bottle to safeguard against spilling.)*

Lenny D. Grozier, Binghamton, NY

Oyster Surprise

Surprise! This little oyster is hiding something special under its shell.

Supplies:

2 heavy duty paper plates
purple and blue watercolor
   paints
paintbrush
glue
circle of pink felt, cut to fit inside
   a plate
white pom-pom

stapler
two 4" pipe cleaners
2 tagboard eyes
black marker
hole puncher

Steps:

1. Use the watercolors to paint the bottom of each plate.
2. Glue the felt to the top of a plate.
3. Glue the pom-pom to the felt. *(Staple the plates together along one side to resemble an oyster shell.)*
4. Draw a pupil on each eye.
5. Glue the end of a pipe cleaner to the back of each eye cutout. Allow time for the glue to dry. *(Hole-punch two holes in the front bottom shell of the oyster. Thread each pipe cleaner through a different hole, and twist it tightly to secure it in place. Bend the pipe cleaners forward slightly to help prop the plates open.)*

adapted from an idea by Roxanne LaBell Dearman—Preschool, Western NC Early Intervention Program for Children Who Are Deaf or Hard of Hearing, Charlotte, NC

Grabby Crab

Youngsters get a grip on refrigerator art with this clever crab. Send each child's finished project home to place on his refrigerator. He can display small pieces of artwork by clipping them in the crab's claws.

Supplies:

8 mini craft sticks
2 mini clothespins
red tempera paint
paintbrush
two 5½" red pipe cleaners
3½" red craft foam circle

hole puncher
black permanent marker
glue
3" adhesive magnet strip

Steps:

1. Paint the craft sticks and clothespins red. Allow time for the paint to dry.
2. Thread an end of each pipe cleaner through the spring on a clothespin and secure it by twisting.
3. Hole-punch two holes in the foam. Thread the remaining end of each pipe cleaner through a hole and secure it by twisting.
4. Use the marker to draw eyes and a mouth.
5. Glue four craft sticks to each side of the bottom of the circle.
6. Attach the magnet to the bottom of the crab. Set the project aside to dry.

Heather Lynn Miller—PreK, Creative Playschool, Auburn, IN

Drippy Seaweed

The result of this activity is a totally unique piece of ocean-themed artwork!

Supplies:

slightly thinned tempera paint in
   shades of green
teaspoon
9" x 12" white construction paper
colorful construction paper

scissors
glue
paintbrush
sand

Supplies:

1. Place small dollops of paint at the bottom of the white paper, alternating shades of green.
2. Tip the paper slightly in different directions to allow the paint to run. Allow time for the paint to dry.
3. Cut out construction paper fish and other sea animal shapes. Glue them to the picture.
4. Brush glue along the bottom of the picture.
5. Sprinkle sand on the glue. Set the project aside to dry.

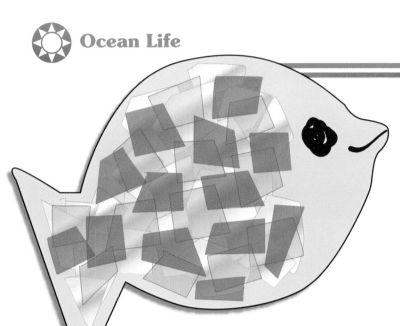

Flashy Fish

Everyone will take notice of this bright and cheerful fish. So display a school of these fancy fellows on a bulletin board or in a hallway.

Supplies:

construction paper fish
black marker
aluminum foil
glue
small pieces of cellophane

Steps:

1. Use a black marker to draw a face on the fish.
2. Tear pieces of aluminum foil and glue them onto the fish.
3. Glue pieces of cellophane over the foil. Set the project aside to dry.

A Room With a View

When youngsters make this mural, they transform a wall of your classroom into a fascinating underwater view!

Supplies:

white bulletin board paper
scissors
construction paper
crayons
tape
blue cellophane

Setup:

Attach a length of bulletin board paper to a wall.

Steps:

1. Cut out ocean plants and animals from construction paper. Color and decorate them as desired.
2. Tape the pictures to the bulletin board paper. *(Tape cellophane over the paper to give the effect of water.)*

Slice of Sunshine

Rays of warmth beam through this sunny card, which is perfect for any occasion.

Supplies:

12" x 18" white construction paper
pencil
5" circle template
yellow and red tempera paint
spoon
paintbrush
plastic toy pizza cutter
crayons

Steps:

1. Fold the paper to make a card.
2. Trace a circle on the card.
3. Spoon a dime-size drop of each color of paint on the circle.
4. Swirl the paint together with a paintbrush.
5. Place the pizza cutter in the center of the circle and roll it out to the edge of the card to make a sunbeam. Repeat until the card is full of sunbeams. Let the paint dry.
6. Open the card and personalize it with crayons.

Roxanne LaBell Dearman—Preschool, Western NC Program for Children Who Are Deaf or Hard of Hearing, Charlotte, NC

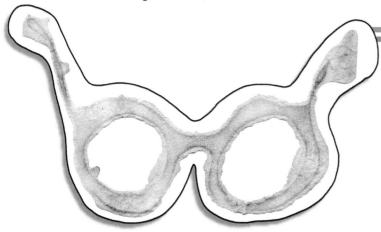

Snazzy Sunglasses

Add sparkle to a door display with these eye-catching sunglasses.

Supplies:

variety of food coloring	glue
dishes of water	salt
eyedroppers	scissors
8" tagboard square	

Setup:

As youngsters observe, mix each different food coloring in a separate bowl of water. Place an eyedropper next to each bowl of colored water.

Steps:

1. Use glue to make a sunglasses shape on the tagboard.
2. Sprinkle salt onto the glue. Remove any excess salt.
3. Use an eyedropper to drip one drop of colored water onto the salt.
   (Encourage youngsters to observe as the salt absorbs the colored water.)
4. Repeat Step 3 with each remaining color until the entire sunglasses shape is colored. Let it dry.
5. Cut around the shape of the sunglasses.

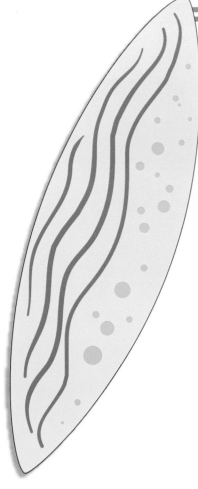

Squirt 'n' Surf

Wax this colorful surfboard and then catch a wave in the dramatic-play center!

Supplies:

colored tagboard
scissors
clean plastic squirt bottles (such as glue or liquid detergent bottles)
glue
tablespoon
assorted colors of tempera paint

Setup:

Cut a tagboard surfboard shape for each small group of students. Partially fill each squirt bottle with glue and then add a tablespoon of paint to each one. Shake each bottle to mix the colored glue. Tell youngsters to pretend that the bottle contains surfboard wax.

Steps:

1. Take turns squeezing wax onto the surfboard to create a cool design. Let it dry.
2. Take off your shoes and step onto the board to pretend to surf on the ocean.

Heather Lynn Miller—PreK, Creative Playschool, Auburn, IN

Sunny Print

Add sunshine to any classroom display with these sunny orange prints.

Supplies:

scissors
yellow and orange construction paper
half of an orange
yellow paint

white construction paper
clear glitter
glue

Setup:

Cut a supply of yellow and orange paper triangles to use for sun rays. Allow the orange half to dry for several hours.

Steps:

1. Dip the orange half in yellow paint and then press a print onto the white paper.
2. Sprinkle the wet paint with glitter. Let it dry.
3. Cut out the print.
4. Glue yellow and orange triangles onto the back of the print to resemble sun rays.

Sandpaper Castles

Bring the beach close to home with these sandy castles.

Supplies:

fine sandpaper
coarse sandpaper
old scissors
9" x 12" blue construction paper
glue
colored chalk
construction paper scraps

Setup:

Cut a supply of fine sandpaper circles, squares, triangles, and rectangles. Cut a supply of coarse sandpaper wave shapes.

Steps:

1. Glue several triangles, circles, rectangles, and squares onto the blue paper to create a sandcastle.
2. Glue several wave shapes along the bottom of the blue paper to create a beach.
3. Use colored chalk to add details.
4. Cut out a construction paper flag and glue it above the castle.

Heather Lynn Miller—PreK, Creative Playschool, Auburn, IN

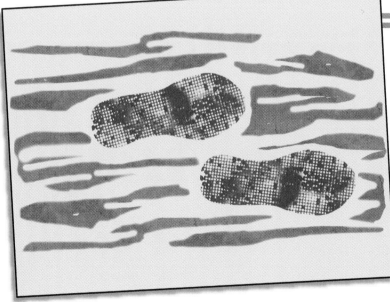

Sandy Stroll

These flip-flops were made for taking a sunny stroll on a sandy beach!

Supplies:

glue
shallow pan (big enough to hold a flip-flop)
rubber flip-flops
tan construction paper
colored sand
uncolored sand

Setup:

Pour glue into the shallow pan.

Steps:

1. Dip the bottom of one flip-flop into the glue.
2. Press a flip-flop print onto the paper.
3. Sprinkle the print with colored sand.
4. Repeat Steps 1–3 with the other flip-flop. Shake off the excess sand.
5. Spread glue around the flip-flop prints.
6. Sprinkle the area with uncolored sand. Let it dry. Shake off the excess sand.

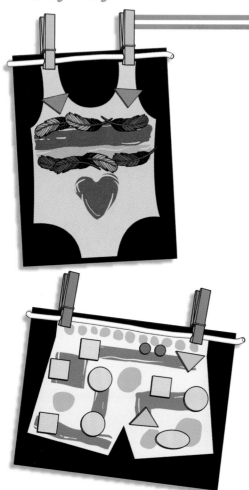

Spectacular Swimsuits

Dive into summer with a full line of swimsuits on display.

Supplies:

9" x 12" colored construction paper
scissors
9" x 12" black construction paper
glue
craft supplies
paint
paintbrushes
10" length of cotton string
2 plastic spring-type clothespins

Setup:

Cut out a swimsuit shape from the colored paper.

Steps:

1. Glue the swimsuit onto the black paper.
2. Decorate the swimsuit with craft supplies and paint as desired.
3. Glue the string along the top of the paper.
4. Clip the clothespins at the top of the swimsuit along the string.

Deborah Ryan—Preschool, Early Head Start Family Center of Portland
Portland, OR

Shimmering Sun

These happy suncatchers are sure to bring smiles to little faces!

Supplies:

plastic margarine lid
Mod Podge mixture
paintbrush
1" yellow tissue paper squares
1" orange tissue paper triangles

construction paper scraps
glue
hole puncher
yellow ribbon

Steps:

1. Brush Mod Podge mixture onto the top of the plastic lid.
2. Layer yellow tissue paper on the lid.
3. Place orange tissue paper around the outer edge of the lid to create sun rays. Let it dry.
4. Glue on paper scraps to make a face.
5. Punch a hole near the edge of the plastic lid.
6. Thread the ribbon through the hole in the lid and tie it in a loop.
7. Brush the project with Mod Podge mixture again. Let it dry.

Sunny Smiles

The smiles won't fade when each youngster creates this bright sun!

Supplies:

yellow food coloring
medium-size dish of water
coffee filter
scissors
permanent marker

Setup:

As youngsters observe, add drops of food coloring to the dish of water until a bright yellow color is achieved.

Steps:

1. Dip the filter into the yellow water.
2. Squeeze the excess water from the filter and lay it flat. Let it dry.
3. Snip one-inch slits around the edge of the coffee filter.
4. Draw a face on the center of the filter with a permanent marker.

Roxanne LaBell Dearman—Preschool, Western NC Early Intervention Program for Children Who Are Deaf or Hard of Hearing, Charlotte, NC

Sandy Pails and Shovels

These sandy pails and shovels will remind you of sunny days and will also make a fun window display!

Supplies:

waxed paper	hole puncher
glue	ribbon
colored sand	

Setup:

Plan to have half the class make sand pails and the other half make sand shovels. Then pair shovels and pails to display in a window.

Steps:

1. Squeeze glue into the shape of a sand pail or a sand shovel onto waxed paper.
2. Sprinkle the shape with colored sand. Let it dry.
3. Gently peel the shape from the waxed paper.
4. Hole-punch the top of the shape.
5. Tie a loop of ribbon on the shape and display it in a window.

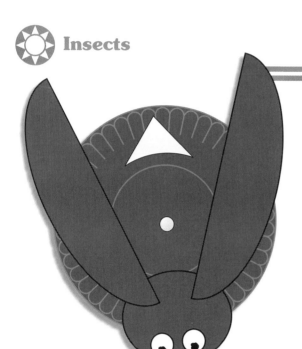

Flashing Firefly

Watch little ones' faces light up when they each make this firefly! To turn the firefly's light on and off, simply rotate the wheel!

Supplies:

scissors
6" paper plate
black tempera paint
paintbrush
glue
3" black construction paper circle (head)

2" x 6" black construction paper crescent shapes (wings)
black and yellow crayons
white construction paper eyes
6" white construction paper circle
brad

Setup:

Cut out a triangle near the edge of the plate.

Steps:

1. Paint the bottom of the plate black. Allow time for the paint to dry.
2. Glue the head to the plate, opposite the triangle.
3. Glue the wings to the plate.
4. Use the black crayon to color pupils on the eyes. Then glue the eyes to the head.
5. Color half of the white circle yellow and the other half black. *(Place the plate on top of the circle. Push the brad through both layers and then secure it in place.)*

Roxanne LaBell Dearman—PreK, Western NC Early Intervention Program for Children Who Are Deaf or Hard of Hearing, Charlotte, NC

Dragonfly Deluxe

Jazz up a pond bulletin board or wall display with this showy dragonfly!

Supplies:

blue and green food coloring
2 partially filled cups of water
paint-stirring stick (body)
blue tempera paint
2 cone-shaped coffee filters, size number 4 (wings)

eyedroppers
paintbrushes
scissors
glue
Elmer's Shimmer 'N Shine art glaze
two 3" pipe cleaners (eyes)

Setup:

Use food coloring to tint each cup of water a different color.

Steps:

1. Paint the body blue.
2. Flatten each coffee filter.
3. Use the eyedroppers to drip tinted water and drops of concentrated food coloring on the filters. Allow time for the filters to dry. Then cut each filter in half, beginning at the point.
4. Glue the wings behind the body.
5. Paint the wings and body with the art glaze.
6. Curl the pipe cleaners and glue them to the head of the dragonfly. Set the project aside to dry.

Ada Goren, Winston-Salem, NC

Bug-Eyed Butterfly

This butterfly may look surprised, but it's really just impressed with your unique use of utensils.

Supplies:

12" x 18" colored construction paper (wings)
scissors
crayons
glue
3" x 9" green construction paper (body)
black permanent marker
2 transparent plastic spoons
transparent tape
½" x 6" construction paper strip
pencil

Setup:

Fold the large construction paper in half and cut butterfly wings.

Steps:

1. Use crayons to decorate the wings.
2. Round the corners of the body.
3. Glue the body to the wings.
4. Use the marker to draw pupils on the spoons to resemble eyes. Then tape the eyes to the body.
5. Curl the paper strip around a pencil. Glue it below the eyes to resemble the butterfly's proboscis.

adapted from an idea by Heather Lynn Miller—PreK, Creative Playschool, Auburn, IN

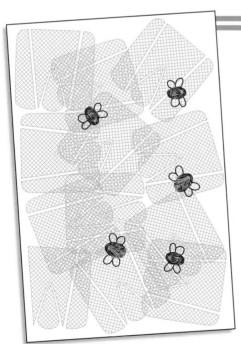

Splat

These flyswatter prints will be a smashing success with your little ones!

Supplies:

unused flyswatter
shallow pan of colorful
    tempera paint
12" x 18" white construction paper
black washable ink pad
fine-tip black marker

Setup:

Consider setting up this project outdoors to make cleanup easier.

Steps:

1. Dip the flyswatter in the pan of colorful paint.
2. Gently swat the paper. Repeat the process several times until a desired effect is achieved. Allow time for the paint to dry.
3. Make black fingerprints on the paper. Allow time for the paint to dry.
4. Use the marker to draw wings on the prints.

Lynn C. Mode—Gr. K, Benton Heights Elementary, Monroe, NC

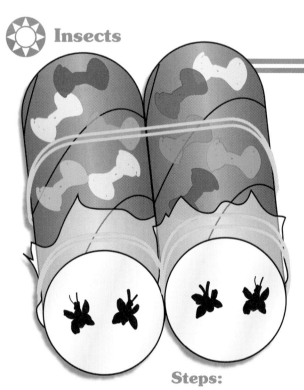

"Bug-noculars"

Beautiful butterflies abound when youngsters look through this bug viewer!

Supplies:

black permanent marker
two 5" squares of plastic wrap
2 small cardboard tubes
tempera paints
paintbrush
3 rubber bands

Setup:

For each child, use the marker to draw two simple butterflies in the middle of each plastic wrap square.

Steps:

1. Paint the cardboard tubes as desired. Allow time for the paint to dry.
2. Wrap a plastic square around the end of each tube and use a rubber band to hold it in place.
3. Bind the tubes together with a rubber band to resemble binoculars.

Lynn C. Mode—Gr. K, Benton Heights Elementary, Monroe, NC

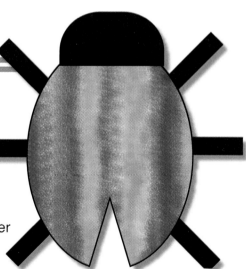

Rainbow Beetles

These shimmering beetles sport stripes in a variety of colors!

Supplies:

9" x 12" white construction paper
metallic tempera paint
colorful tempera paint
sponge paint rollers
scissors

glue
3" x 4" black construction paper
(head)
six 2" x 3" black construction paper
strips (legs)

Steps:

1. Drizzle rows of paint on the paper. Roll the paint roller back and forth across the paper until a desired effect is achieved. Allow time for the paint to dry. *(Cut a beetle body shape from the paper.)*
2. Round two corners of the beetle head. Glue the head to one end.
3. Flip the beetle on its back. Glue on six legs.
4. Set the project aside to dry.

Deborah Ryan—Preschool, Early Head Start Family Center of Portland, Portland, OR

Gigantic Butterfly

This super-size butterfly looks lovely hanging in a classroom. Simply tie monofilament around the cardboard tube and then hang it from your ceiling.

Supplies:

large cardboard tube
green tempera paint
paintbrush
2 sheets of colorful tissue paper
stapler
pipe cleaner

Steps:

1. Paint the tube green. Allow time for the paint to dry.
2. Stack the sheets of tissue paper, gather the sheets in the middle, and then twist them together to resemble wings. *(Staple the wings to the tube.)*
3. Bend the pipe cleaner to resemble antennae. *(Staple the antennae to the top of the tube.)*

Deborah Ryan—Preschool, Early Head Start Family Center of Portland, Portland, OR

Ladybug on a Leaf

When youngsters make this adorable ladybug, you're sure to spot them enjoying themselves!

Supplies:

9" x 12" green construction paper leaf
¼ of an apple
red tempera paint
black tempera paint

Steps:

1. Make two red apple prints side by side on the leaf to resemble a ladybug. Allow time for the paint to dry.
2. Use a finger to paint a black line down the middle of the ladybug.
3. Make black fingerprint spots.
4. Make a black fingerprint head.
5. Use a finger to paint six black legs.

adapted from an idea by Lenny D. Grozier, Binghamton, NY

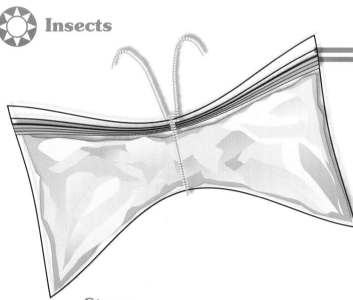

Lovely Luna Moth

Enjoyment is in the bag when little ones make this luna moth. Display the moths on a bulletin board decorated like the night sky.

Supplies:

2 sheets of copy paper
paintbrush
light green tempera paint
white bumpy chenille stem
snack-size resealable plastic bag

Steps:

1. Paint the sheets of paper light green. Allow time for the sheets to dry.
2. Crumple the sheets so the painted side faces outward. Then place them in the plastic bag.
3. Wrap the chenille stem around the middle of the bag to form wings.
4. Adjust the ends of the stem to resemble antennae.

Rebecca Pries—Three-Year-Olds, The Sunshine House, Charlotte, NC

A Honey of a Bee

This paper plate craft is perfect for your classroom of busy little bees!

Supplies:

small paper plate
black and yellow tempera paint
paintbrush
white construction paper eyes

black marker
glue
black construction paper stinger
waxed paper wings

Steps:

1. Paint alternating black and yellow stripes on the plate. Allow time for the paint to dry.
2. Use the black marker to draw pupils on the eyes. Glue the eyes to the plate.
3. Glue the stinger to the plate.
4. Glue the wings to the back of the plate.

Heather Lynn Miller—PreK, Creative Playschool, Auburn, IN

Beginner Butterfly

Youngsters use a beginner pencil to add colorful dots of paint to this butterfly.

Supplies:

white construction paper butterfly
   with section dividers
crayon
beginner pencils
shallow pans of colorful
   tempera paint

Setup:

Place a beginner pencil next to each pan of paint.

Steps:

1. Use a crayon to color the butterfly's body.
2. Dip the eraser end of a pencil into the paint and print dots on the butterfly's wings, taking care to make the butterfly symmetrical. Set the project aside to dry.

Stacy Wingen—Gr. K, Howard Elementary, Howard, SD

Chirpy

This cute little cricket is "eggs-tra" special!

Supplies:

black tempera paint
white glue
3-segment section of a foam egg
   carton, cleaned and sanitized
paintbrush
2 construction paper legs
black construction paper heart
two 3" black pipe cleaners
black marker
white construction paper eyes

Setup:

To make paint that adheres to foam, mix two parts glue with one part black tempera paint.

Steps:

1. Brush a thick layer of paint on the bottom of the egg carton. Allow time for the paint to dry.
2. Glue a leg to each side of the carton.
3. Fold the heart in half. Glue it to the top of the cricket to resemble wings.
4. Poke the pipe cleaners into the front segment. Then curve them to resemble antennae.
5. Draw pupils on the eyes. Glue them under the antennae.

Swirly, Whirly Tie

This simple Father's Day gift won't tie up a big portion of your day!

Supplies:

colorful fingerpaint
plastic spoons
12" x 18" white construction paper
scissors
marker

Setup:

Place spoonfuls of colorful fingerpaint on each child's paper.

Step:

Use your fingers to briefly swirl the paints. Allow time for the paint to dry. *(Cut a tie shape from the paper. Write "Happy Father's Day!" on the tie.)*

adapted from an idea by Ada Goren, Winston-Salem, NC

Give Dad a Hand

Warm hearts with this handsome card!

Supplies:

9" x 12" construction paper
shallow pan of tempera paint
small construction paper heart
glue
copy of the poem shown
marker

Setup:

Fold the paper to make a card.

Steps:

1. Press your hand in the paint and then on the card cover. Allow time for the paint to dry.
2. Make a similar handprint on the inside of the card. Allow time for the paint to dry.
3. Glue the heart on the handprint inside the card.
4. Glue the first three lines of the poem on the front of the card.
5. Glue the last three lines of the poem inside the card.
6. Sign the card.

Heather Lynn Miller—PreK, Creative Playschool, Auburn, IN

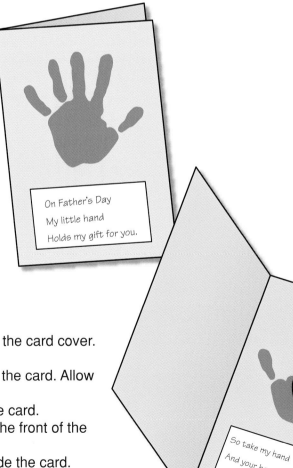

On Father's Day
My little hand
Holds my gift for you.

So take my hand
And your heart will melt
With love that's warm and true!

Tyreece

112

Fabulous Foil Paintings

Fathers will take a shine to this artsy child-made gift!

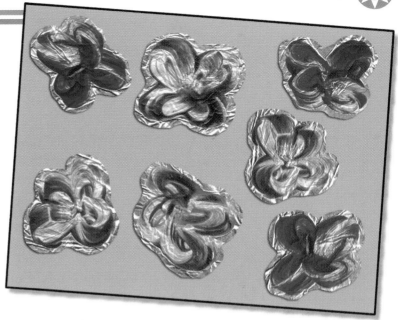

Supplies:
8" x 10" piece of heavy-duty foil
tempera paint
paintbrush
2 sheets of 9" x 12" construction paper
scissors
glue

Steps:
1. Paint individual objects or designs on the foil. Allow time for the paint to dry.
2. Glue the foil to a sheet of construction paper. Let the glue dry.
3. Cut around your designs.
4. Glue them to the other sheet of paper.

Deborah Ryan—Preschool, Early Head Start Family Center of Portland, Portland, OR

Picture-Perfect

The dad who receives this frame and picture is sure to know he's "thumb-body" special!

Supplies:
four 6" tongue depressors
glue
shallow pans of tempera paint
5" x 5" white construction paper
crayons

Steps:
1. Glue the tongue depressors together to make a square frame.
2. Make colorful fingerprints and thumbprints on the frame. Allow time for the glue and paint to dry.
3. Use crayons to draw on the paper a picture of yourself with your father or other special caregiver.
4. Glue the paper to the back of the frame.

Heather Lynn Miller—PreK, Creative Playschool, Auburn, IN

Hammer Painting

This process-oriented art activity is sure to be a hit with your little carpenters!

Supplies:

plastic toy hammer
shallow pans of tempera paint
9" x 12" white construction paper
scissors
12" x 18" sheet of construction paper, folded in half
glue
marker

Steps:

1. Dip the hammer in a pan of paint.
2. Gently pound the hammer on the white paper.
3. Repeat the process with other colors of paint. Allow time for the paint to dry. *(Cut a heart shape from the paper.)*
4. Glue the heart to the outside of the folded paper to make a card. *(Encourage each child to dictate a message to her father as you write her words on the inside of the card.)*
5. Write your name inside the card.

Roxanne LaBell Dearman—Preschool, Western North Carolina Early Intervention Program for Children Who Are Deaf or Hard of Hearing, Charlotte, NC

King for a Day

Give fathers the royal treatment with this crown! For a day of attention fit for a king, each father adjusts the crown to fit his head and then secures it with the provided paper clip!

Supplies:

6" x 27" yellow paper, cut to resemble a crown
sticky dots
crayons
paper clip

Steps:

1. Write "Dad the King" on the paper.
2. Use the sticky dots and crayons to decorate the paper. *(Roll the paper to resemble a crown, securing it with a paper clip.)*

Roxanne LaBell Dearman—Preschool

Have a Hug

Your little ones will embrace this playful project with open arms!

Supplies:

skin-tone construction paper circle
crayons
construction paper scraps
sentence strip
black marker
2 skin-tone construction paper hands
glue

Steps:

1. Use the crayons and scraps to add features to the circle so that it resembles your face. *(Have each child dictate a short message to her father while you write her words on the sentence strip.)*
2. Sign your name on the sentence strip.
3. Glue the face and two hands to the sentence strip. Allow time for the glue to dry.
4. Fold the hands in before delivering the message to your dad.

Dad Is "Gr8"

This vanity plate says it all! Fathers will love receiving a car-themed project for this special day!

Supplies:

12" x 18" construction paper
scissors
crayons
4" x 6" piece of copy paper, folded in half (card)
black marker
glue

Setup:

For each child, cut a shape from the construction paper that resembles the rear view of a car. Draw a window on each cutout. Write "Dad is Gr8!" on the folded paper. (Depending on each child's situation, you may want to replace "Dad" with another caregiver's name or title.)

Steps:

1. Use crayons to draw a picture of yourself in the window and then decorate the car as desired. *(Have each child dictate a message to his father or caregiver; write the message on the inside of the card.)*
2. Glue the card to the car.

Autographs, Please!

Wrap up the end of the school year with an autograph party!

Supplies:

8½" x 11" drawing paper
markers
11" x 18" construction paper
glue

Steps:

1. Draw a picture of your school.
2. Glue the drawing in the center of the construction paper.
3. Write the grade and year across the top of the paper.
4. Ask each classmate to write his or her name on the construction paper around the drawing.

Heather Lynn Miller—PreK, Creative Playschool, Auburn, IN

Memory Book

This school memory book makes a treasured parent gift.

Supplies:

3-hole puncher
two 9" x 12" sheets of craft foam
craft supplies
glue
several plastic sheet protectors
3 binder rings or ribbon strips

Setup:

Punch three holes in the craft foam sheets as shown.

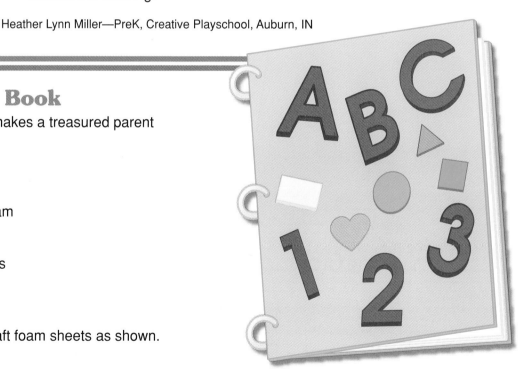

Steps:

1. Use craft supplies to decorate one sheet of craft foam for the book cover. Let it dry.
2. Stack the cover on top of several sheet protectors and the other sheet of craft foam.
3. Assemble the book with binder rings or tie it together with ribbons.
4. Fill the scrapbook with favorite drawing and writing projects by slipping them into sheet protectors. Add sheet protectors as needed.

Lenny D. Grozier, Binghamton, NY

Friendship Quilt

This is a "hand-some" keepsake that makes a beautiful display.

Supplies:

6" square of craft foam
scissors
8" square of white tagboard
eight 2" squares of colored
  paper

eight 2" squares of
  patterned paper
glue
hole puncher
yarn

Setup:

Trace a child's hand onto the foam and cut it out.

Steps:

1. Arrange the squares of colored and patterned paper on the tagboard. Glue each square in place to make a quilt block.
2. Glue the foam handprint in the middle of the quilt block. Let the glue dry.
3. Punch holes around the outer edge.
4. Lace yarn through the holes to finish the block.

Lenny D. Grozier, Binghamton, NY

Memory Magnet

These magnets make great end-of-school parent gifts.

Supplies:

craft foam
scissors
child's photo
3" poster board square

tacky glue
craft foam scraps
magnetic tape

Setup:

Cut the craft foam into a desired shape (no larger than three inches). Cut an oval in the center of the foam sized to frame the photo.

Steps:

1. Glue the photo onto the middle of the poster board.
2. Spread glue onto the poster board area surrounding the photo.
3. Center the frame over the photo and press it down to attach the two pieces. Let it dry. *(Trim away the excess poster board.)*
4. Use foam scraps to decorate the frame.
5. Attach a strip of magnetic tape to the back of the frame.

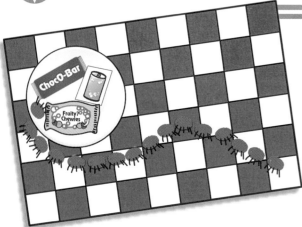

Pesky Picnic Pals

Invite your youngsters to combine their finished projects for a precious picnic picture!

Supplies:

twenty-seven 2" red construction paper squares
12" x 18" white construction paper
glue

weekly grocery advertisements
scissors
small paper plate
black washable stamp pad
black marker

Steps:

1. Glue the red squares to the white paper to resemble a checkered tablecloth.
2. Cut pictures of picnic foods from the advertisements. Glue them to the plate.
3. Glue the plate to the tablecloth. Let the glue dry.
4. Make a row of black fingerprints over the tablecloth to represent ants.
5. Add legs to each ant.

Roxanne LaBell Dearman—PreK, Western NC Early Intervention Program for Children Who Are Deaf or Hard of Hearing, Charlotte, NC

Summer Produce People

Summer's fruits and vegetables are tasty and oh so inspiring. Go ahead—play with this food!

Supplies:

construction paper fruits and vegetables
glue
markers

Steps:

1. Assemble the fruits and vegetables in the shape of a person.
2. Glue them together. Let the glue dry.
3. Add details and facial features with markers.

Dawn Rolita—Gr. K, World Cup Nursery School and Kindergarten, Chappaqua, NY

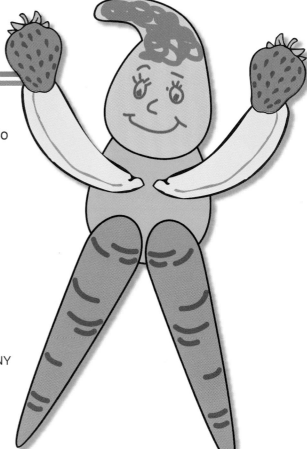

Great Grapes!

Sweet, juicy grapes are a classic summer fruit. Enjoy printing a bunch with your bunch!

Supplies:

light-colored construction paper
cork
shallow dish of purple or
   light green tempera paint
brown marker

green construction paper
   grape leaf
green curling ribbon
scissors
glue

Steps:

1. Dip the cork into the paint.
2. Print a cluster of grapes on your paper. Let the paint dry.
3. Draw a stem.
4. Put the ribbon under the leaf so that the ends stick out, and glue the leaf to the stem. *(Curl the ribbon.)*

Deborah Ryan—Preschool, Early Head Start Family Center of Portland, Portland, OR

Fresh Fruit Salad

A mouthwatering plateful of fruit salad makes a healthy, artistic display when you mount each plate on a tablecloth-covered bulletin board.

Supplies:

magazines
scissors
paper plate

glue
plastic fork

Steps:

1. Cut out pictures of fruits from a magazine.
2. Glue the fruit pictures on your plate.
3. Glue the fork beside your favorite fruit. Let the glue dry.

Deborah Ryan—Preschool

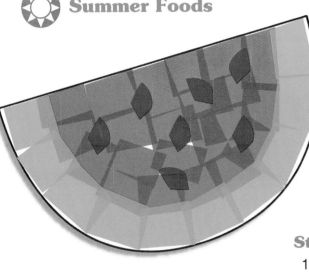

A Slice of Summer

Everybody's yellin' for watermelon!

Supplies:

12"-wide tagboard half circle
1" squares of red and green tissue paper
water-thinned glue
old paintbrush
7 black tissue paper seeds

Steps:

1. Brush glue on the rounded edge of your half circle.
2. Cover the glue with green tissue paper to resemble a watermelon rind.
3. Brush glue on the center of your watermelon slice.
4. Cover the glue with red tissue paper to resemble watermelon flesh.
5. Glue on the seeds.
6. Brush glue over the entire slice. Set it aside to dry.

Lynn C. Mode—Gr. K, Benton Heights Elementary, Monroe, NC

Precious Pineapples

This bright-colored pineapple is sure to be welcome anywhere!

Supplies:

tan construction paper oval
small triangular sponge
shallow tray of yellow tempera paint

long triangles of green construction paper
glue

Steps:

1. Print rows of triangles on the oval. Let the paint dry.
2. Glue on the green triangles to resemble a pineapple top.

Ice Pop Painting

Think cool. Think refreshing. Think paint? When an ice pop is your paintbrush, some pretty effects are possible!

Supplies:

4" x 6" white construction paper   craft stick
ice pop   glue
scissors

Steps:

1. Paint the paper with the ice pop. Set it aside to dry.
2. Cut an ice pop shape from the painting.
3. Glue a craft stick to the back.

Gail Marsh—Preschool and Pre-Kindergarten, St. Mark's Lutheran School, Eureka, MO

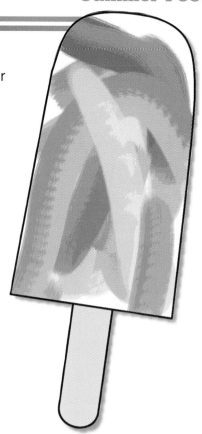

Ice-Cream Soda

This mouthwatering masterpiece has real taste appeal!

Supplies:

soda glass sketched on white construction paper
glue
watercolor paints
paintbrush
scissors

12" x 18" colorful construction paper
shallow tray of white tempera paint
sponge
cotton balls
half drinking straw

Steps:

1. Squeeze glue to outline the soda glass. Let the glue dry.
2. Paint the inside of the glass. Let the paint dry.
3. Cut out the glass and glue it to the colored paper.
4. Sponge-print an ice-cream scoop on top of the glass.
5. Pull apart cotton balls and glue them to the rim of the glass.
6. Glue the straw in place.

Ice-Cream Sundaes

This keepsake sundae is perfect for each child's art gallery on the refrigerator at home!

Supplies:

nonmenthol shaving cream
white glue
large bowl
mixing spoon
9" x 12" construction paper
4" tan, pink, and white
   construction paper circles
   (ice-cream scoops)

brown-tinted glue
   (chocolate syrup)
red-tinted glue
   (strawberry syrup)
pom-pom (cherry)
1" x 12" construction
   paper strip (bowl)
scissors

Setup:

Mix equal parts shaving cream and white glue in the bowl to make whipped-cream paint.

Steps:

1. Glue the ice-cream scoops to the paper.
2. Drizzle syrup over the ice cream.
3. Add dollops of whipped cream to the sundae.
4. Top with a cherry.
5. Round two corners of the bowl and glue it on.

Coramarie Marinan—Gr. K, Howe School, Green Bay, WI

Cotton Candy

This rendition of a childhood favorite is great for an end-of-the-year carnival. Plus, it's not even a bit sticky!

Supplies:

white tagboard
water-thinned glue
old paintbrush
cotton balls

scissors
spray bottles of thinned
   tempera paint
tagboard triangle (cone)

Steps:

1. Paint glue on the tagboard.
2. Stretch cotton balls and stick them to the glue. Let the glue dry. *(Cut around the shape of the cotton.)*
3. Lightly spray-paint the cotton to resemble cotton candy. Hang to dry.
4. Glue the cotton candy to the cone.

Red, White, Blue, and You!

This patriotic placemat is just right for an all-American snacktime!

Supplies:
12" x 18" blue construction paper
assorted red and white construction
  paper strips
metallic streamers
assorted star stickers or die-cuts
glue

Steps:
1. Randomly glue the strips and streamers to the blue paper.
2. Add stars where desired. Set it aside to dry. *(Laminate the placemat.)*

Angie Kutzer—Gr. K, Garrett Elementary School
Mebane, NC

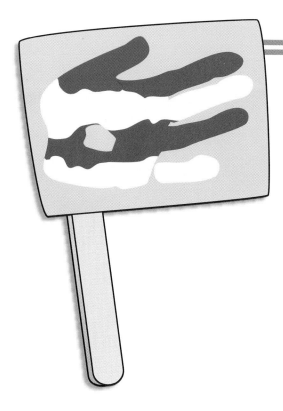

Patriotic Palms

These handsome little flags will be the pride of your holiday parade!

Supplies:
red, white, and blue washable tempera paint
3 paintbrushes
5" x 7" light blue construction paper
scissors
jumbo craft stick
glue

Setup:
Paint the thumb of a child's right hand blue. Paint the fingers and palm with alternating stripes of red and white.

Steps:
1. Press the hand onto the paper and lift it straight up. Set the print aside to dry.
2. Cut out a rectangle around the print so it resembles a flag.
3. Glue the flag to the craft stick.

Heather Lynn Miller—PreK, Creative Playschool, Auburn, IN **123**

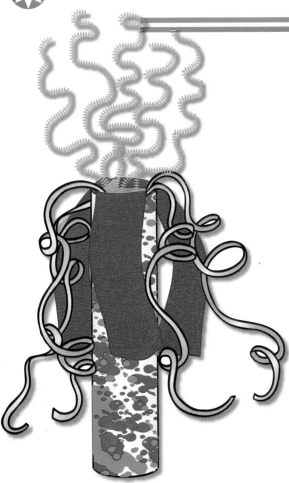

Sparkly Wand

What's red, white, sparkly, and blue? A patriotic project that's fun to do!

Supplies:

paper towel tube
paintbrush
white, red, and blue tempera paint
two 14" squares of waxed paper
red crepe paper streamers
strips of metallic curling ribbon
4 metallic pipe cleaners
stapler
glue
pencil
scissors

Steps:

1. Paint the tube white. Let the paint dry.
2. Fingerpaint a design in red paint on waxed paper.
3. Roll the tube over the design. Let the paint dry.
4. Fingerpaint a design in blue paint on the other square of waxed paper.
5. Roll the tube over the design. Let the paint dry.
6. Bundle together a few lengths of streamers, some ribbon, and the pipe cleaners. Staple the bundle at one end.
7. Squeeze some glue around the inside on one end of the tube.
8. Push the stapled end of the streamer bundle into the glued end of the tube. Let the glue dry.
9. Curl the pipe cleaners around a pencil. *(Curl the ribbon.)*

Ada Goren, Winston-Salem, NC

Fourth of July Fireworks

Ooh! Aah! A display of these breathtaking collages will resemble a grand fireworks finale!

Supplies:

metallic collage supplies (tinsel, wrapping paper, doilies, ribbon)
black construction paper
scissors
glue

Setup:

Cut the collage materials into manageable sizes.

Steps:

1. Arrange the collage materials on the paper. Cut or tear to fit.
2. Glue the collage to the paper. Set it aside to dry.

Deborah Ryan—Preschool, Early Head Start Family Center of Portland, Portland, OR

Anytime

Little Lava Lamp

Shake up your young scientists by explaining that oil and water don't mix. Then let them test the idea by completing this clever craft!

Supplies:

funnel
clean, empty, clear plastic water
   or soda bottle
water
food coloring
baby oil
glitter or confetti (optional)
bright-colored electrical tape

Steps:

1. Use the funnel to fill the bottle half-full with water.
2. Add food coloring. Recap and shake.
3. Use the funnel to add baby oil until the bottle is full. *(If desired, add glitter or confetti.)*
4. Replace the lid and seal tightly with electrical tape.

Lenny D. Grozier, Binghamton, NY

Peekaboo Picture

Post these translucent face pictures in your window and let the sun shine in. Your classroom will be all smiles!

Supplies:

9" x 12" construction paper
scissors
8" x 11" skin-colored tissue paper
glue
markers
yarn

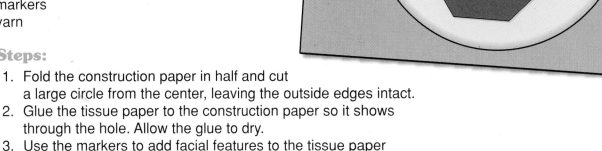

Steps:

1. Fold the construction paper in half and cut a large circle from the center, leaving the outside edges intact.
2. Glue the tissue paper to the construction paper so it shows through the hole. Allow the glue to dry.
3. Use the markers to add facial features to the tissue paper and glue on the yarn for hair.

Robin McClay—PreK and Gr. K Centers, St. Joseph Institute for the Deaf, Chesterfield, MO

Oh-So-Pretty Placemats

Snacktime will be a fun time with these swirly placemats!

Supplies:

2 tbsp. clear corn syrup
8" x 10" white tagboard
food coloring

Steps:

1. Pour the corn syrup onto one area of the tagboard and spread it with your hands.
2. Squeeze one drop of food coloring onto the corn syrup. Watch the color spread and grow.
3. Repeat Steps 1 and 2 with other sections of the tagboard. Let it dry for several days. *(Laminate the placemat.)*

Robin McClay—PreK and Gr. K Centers, St. Joseph Institute for the Deaf, Chesterfield, MO

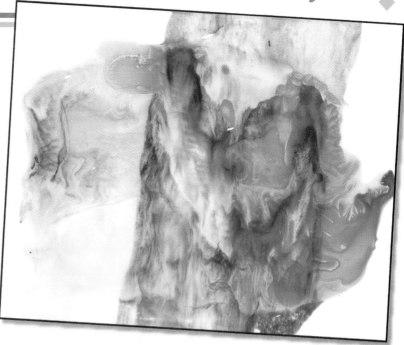

Star-Quality Shapes

One pentagon plus five triangles equals a beautiful star! This star-studded activity features built-in practice with shapes and numbers.

Supplies:

construction paper pentagons in assorted colors
construction paper triangles in assorted colors (each triangle's base must be the same length as one side of the pentagon)
9" x 12" black construction paper
glue

Steps:

1. Glue a pentagon onto the black paper.
2. Glue a triangle beside each side of the pentagon to make a star.
3. Repeat Steps 1 and 2 as space allows.

Lenny D. Grozier, Binghamton, NY

Picassos in Training

These mini masterpieces are packed with lessons about circles, rectangles, and colors.

Supplies:

9" x 12" white construction paper
1" x 12" black construction paper strips
glue
scissors
construction paper circles in assorted sizes and
   colors

Steps:

1. Glue the paper strips onto the white paper to create a design.
2. Trim paper strips that hang over the edge.
3. Glue on the paper circles.

Lenny D. Grozier, Binghamton, NY

Stole-Your-Heart Picture Frame

Create these stained glass–style frames to feature photos of little ones who are near and dear.

Supplies:

two 6" x 8" pieces of clear Con-Tact paper
photograph, trimmed into a heart shape
2" x 2" squares of tissue paper in assorted colors
scissors
hole punch
mini suction hook

Steps:

1. Lay one sheet of Con-Tact paper sticky side up. Place the photo facedown in the center.
2. Arrange squares of tissue paper on the Con-Tact paper to create a design. *(Carefully place the other piece of Con-Tact paper atop the project and seal the edges.)*
3. Trim the Con-Tact paper into a heart shape.
4. Punch a hole in the top of the frame. Use the mini suction hook to hang the frame.

Lenny D. Grozier

Mosaic Mat

Add a burst of color to snacktime with these pretty placemats!

Supplies:

8" x 10" white paper
black marker
ruler
2" tissue paper squares
glue

Steps:

1. Use the ruler to draw a grid of two-inch squares on the white paper.
2. Glue one tissue paper square into each grid space. Allow to dry. *(Laminate.)*

Lenny D. Grozier, Binghamton, NY

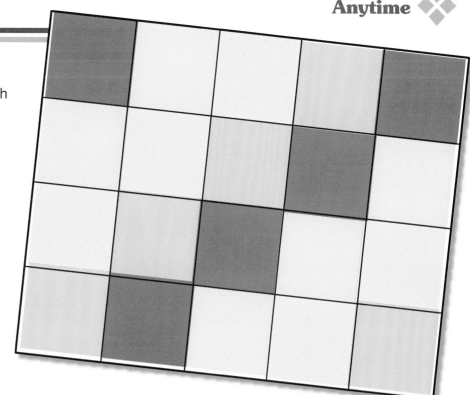

Serene Barnyard Scene

Want to visit the farm without leaving your classroom? This cute craft will set the scene!

Supplies:

9" x 12" white construction paper
crayons
1" x 12" brown construction paper strips
glue
scissors

Steps:

1. On the white paper, draw a barnyard scene that includes different animals.
2. Glue the brown paper strips together to make a fence. Trim as needed.
3. Glue the fence to the white paper.

Circles of Color

Dig out your classroom record player for this versatile craft. The colorful circles can become race car wheels, planets, bubbles—let your imagination run wild!

Supplies:

record album   tape
12" square of white paper   record player
pencil   markers
scissors

Setup:

Trace the album onto the white paper. Cut out the resulting shape and tape it to the album.

Steps:

1. Place the paper-covered album on the record player. Hold a marker so that it's touching the paper. Turn on the record player. Keep the marker in place as the record spins.
2. Place another marker in a different spot on the paper. Repeat several times.

Robin McClay—PreK and Gr. K Centers, St. Joseph Institute for the Deaf, Chesterfield, MO

Fingerprint Fun

Show your little ones how to turn their fingerprints into fine art. Now that's truly a hands-on activity!

Supplies:

washable ink pads
drawing paper
markers

Steps:

1. Press one finger on an ink pad and then on the paper. Repeat with different colors.
2. Use markers to add details.

Robin McClay

My flower is growing in the rain.

Fishy Fun

Fishing around for a unique painting project? This one's "reel-y" fun! Post the completed fish on a bulletin board titled "Our Class Is a Great Catch!"

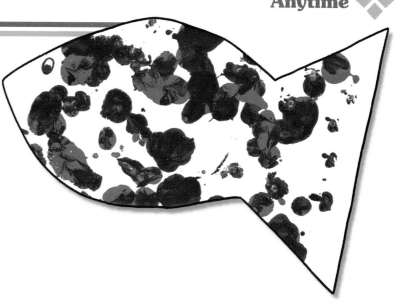

Supplies:

shallow dishes of tempera paint
glitter
Ping-Pong ball or other small ball
construction paper
scissors

Setup:

Add glitter to the paint.

Step:

Use the ball to dab different colors of paint and glitter around the paper. *(Cut the paper into a simple fish shape.)*

Sue Riehl—Preschool, Ross Preschool, Port Huron, MI

Fun-Time Dots

No-fuss materials let students' creativity explode!

Supplies:

9" x 12" construction paper
colored hole reinforcers

Step:

Attach hole reinforcers in a design on the construction paper.

Jill Davis—Grs. K–1 Multiage, Kendall-Whittier Elementary, Tulsa, OK

Toying With Texture

Creativity is sure to rub off on your students when they make these textured crayon rubbings using handy classroom objects.

Supplies:

white paper
assorted crayons with the wrappers removed
small, flat objects such as lace, string, a
   comb, etc.

Steps:

1. Place an object under the paper.
2. Rub the side of the crayon over the paper.
3. Repeat with other items.

Robin McClay—PreK and Gr. K Centers,
St. Joseph Institute for the Deaf, Chesterfield, MO

Common Object Prints

Here's another way to explore the textures on classroom items. This time the trick is to use them to make prints!

Supplies:

shallow dishes of tempera paint
sponges
white paper
small objects that are disposable or can be washed off

Steps:

1. Dab a sponge in a paint dish to get a light coating.
2. Dab a textured item on the sponge and then press it onto the white paper.
3. Repeat with other items.

Robin McClay

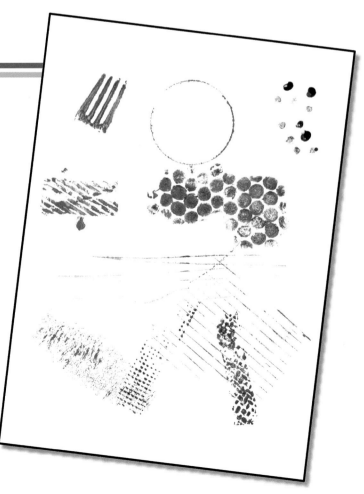

Crafty Collages

Put paper scraps to good use with this creative and inexpensive cut-and-glue project!

Supplies:

scissors
colored construction paper scraps
8½" x 11" white paper
glue
crayons

Steps:

1. Cut paper scraps into desired shapes.
2. Glue the shapes onto the white paper. Add crayon details.

Robin McClay—PreK and Gr. K Centers,
St. Joseph Institute for the Deaf, Chesterfield, MO

Art That Pops off the Page

Create interesting three-dimensional projects using just basic supplies. Little hands will love the textures!

Supplies:

several bottles of white school glue
assorted food coloring
pencil
8½" x 11" sheet of white paper

Setup:

Add several drops of food coloring to a bottle of glue. Use the pencil to mix. Repeat to make several colors.

Step:

Squeeze the glue onto the white paper to make a design. Allow the glue to dry.

Robin McClay

Everyday Clay Play

Little hands will dig right into this simple clay recipe. Plus, it's inexpensive to make so you can enjoy clay play any day!

Supplies:

2 c. flour
2 c. salt
¾ c. plus 2 tbsp. water
bowl
spoon

assorted craft items such as sticks, feathers, or pipe cleaners
large paper clip
markers
12" length of yarn

Setup:

Combine the flour, salt, and ¾ cup water in the bowl. Stir well, adding the additional water if needed. Knead until the clay isn't sticky. Recipe makes enough clay for 12 children.

Steps:

1. Mold clay into a desired shape. Add sticks, feathers, pipe cleaners, or other items. *(Press the paper clip halfway into the clay.)* Allow the clay to dry.
2. Decorate with markers.
3. Thread the yarn through the paper clip and tie to make a hanger.

Robin McClay—PreK and Gr. K Centers, St. Joseph Institute for the Deaf, Chesterfield, MO

Fingerpaint Fun

Do students' papers sometimes tear when they're fingerpainting? This clever technique keeps papers intact and gets creativity flowing!

Supplies:

assorted fingerpaint
plastic serving tray or cafeteria tray
fingerpaint paper

Steps:

1. Place a scoop of fingerpaint on the tray. Use your hands to spread it around.
2. Create a design in the paint.
3. Gently place the paper on top of the design. Press lightly to transfer the design from the tray onto the paper. Lift the paper off the tray and allow it to dry.

Robin McClay

Block-Print Bonanza

Put your old wooden blocks to a new use with this activity. It'll stack up to be lots of fun!

Supplies:

assorted wooden blocks
assorted colors of tempera paint
paintbrushes
7½" x 9" construction paper
9" x 12" construction paper
stapler

Steps:

1. Choose a block. Use the paintbrush to apply paint to one side.
2. Press the block onto the 7½" x 9" piece of paper to create a design. Repeat.
3. Staple the finished project on the 9" x 12" sheet of paper to create a frame.

Deborah Ryan—Preschool, Early Head Start Family Center of Portland, Portland, OR

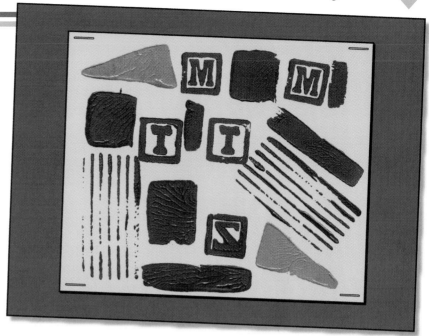

In the Fold

Folding, twisting, taping, looping—challenge students to find creative ways to turn paper strips into 3-D art!

Supplies:

6" x 9" cardboard
paper strips in assorted colors and sizes
tape

Step:

Tape paper strips to the tagboard, accordion-folding or looping the paper to add as much dimension as possible.

Dawn Rolita—Gr. K, World Cup Nursery School and Kindergarten, Chappaqua, NY

135

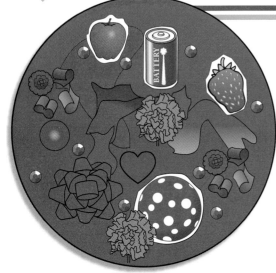

Color Wheel Collage

Color mastery is the focus when each child completes this pretty single-color collage. After you've made collages for each color, make collages shaped to match seasonal themes.

Supplies:

variety of paper in desired color (wallpaper, construction paper, tissue paper, etc.)
scissors
magazines
craft items in desired color
paper plate in desired color
glue

Steps:

1. Cut or tear the papers into small pieces.
2. Cut out magazine pictures in desired color.
3. Glue the paper pieces, pictures, and craft items to the plate. Allow time for the glue to dry.

Jennifer Schear—Preschool, Clover Patch Preschool, Cedar Falls, IA

Rectangle Rodeo Horse

A little buckaroo will have fun making this simple horse!

Supplies:

yarn
scissors
ruler
3" x 6" tan, white, or brown poster board (body)
two 1½" x 3" tan, white, or brown poster board pieces (head and neck)
glue
marker
2 spring-type clothespins

Setup:

Cut yarn into half-inch lengths for the mane and three-inch lengths for the tail.

Steps:

1. Glue the head and neck to the body. Allow time for the glue to dry.
2. Draw facial features.
3. Glue the mane to the back of the neck.
4. Glue the tail to the body. Allow time for the glue to dry.
5. Clip clothespin legs to the body.

Katherine Rickin—Preschool, Mather Child Care, Cleveland, OH

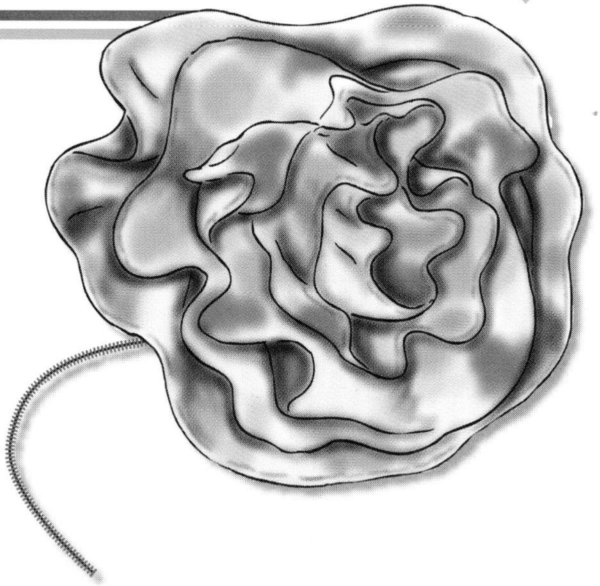

Fluffy Filter Flower

With a quick change of color choice, these flowers can fit into almost any season!

Supplies:

4 coffee filters
stapler
watercolors
paintbrush
green pipe cleaner (stem)

Setup:

Staple four coffee filters together in the center for each child.

Steps:

1. Paint the coffee filters with watercolors. Allow time for the paint to dry.
2. Pull up each coffee filter layer separately and scrunch to form flower petals. Staple a stem to the blossom.

Nancy M. Lotzer—Preschool, The Hillcrest Academy, Dallas, TX

Circle Art

The possibilities are endless with this circle-inspired painting activity!

Supplies:

cardboard tubes
tempera paint in various colors
9" x 12" white construction paper
markers

Steps:

1. Dip the end of a cardboard tube in paint.
2. Make circle prints on white paper. Allow time for the paint to dry.
3. Add details with markers to complete a picture.

Initial Art

Have each youngster complete a craft that is centered around his initials!

Supplies:

alphabet stencils
wallpaper samples
pencil
scissors
glue
9" x 12" black construction paper

Steps:

1. Locate the letter stencils that represent your initials.
2. Select a wallpaper sample.
3. Position the stencils on the wallpaper.
4. Trace around the stencils.
5. Cut out the letters.
6. Glue the letters to the black paper to show your initials.

Stacy Wingen—Gr. K, Howard Elementary, Howard, SD

Piggy Pencil Topper

What student wouldn't want to practice writing with one of these cute piggy pencils!

Supplies:

small ball of pink Crayola Model Magic modeling compound
pencil
black permanent marker

Steps:

1. Use the modeling compound to mold a pig's face with ears and a snout on the eraser end of the pencil. Allow the compound to dry overnight.
2. Use the marker to draw eyes and nostrils.

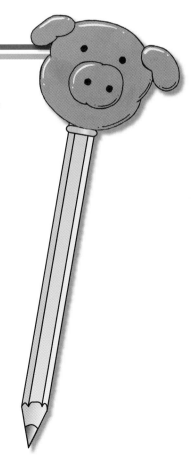

Extra Large Image Art

This idea helps groups of youngsters produce unique works of art!

Supplies:

overhead projector
white bulletin board paper
tape
simple shape outline on an overhead transparency
markers
craft items
variety of paper (construction paper scraps, tissue paper, wallpaper, etc.)
glue

Setup:

For each small group, tape a piece of bulletin board paper to a wall. Set up your overhead projector and place the transparency on it so that it projects onto the paper.

Steps:

1. Use markers to outline the image.
2. Glue craft items and paper pieces to the white paper to fill in the projected image.

Vesta Watkins—Preschool, Good Shepherd Preschool, Blaine, MN

Yarn Painting

This color-mixing activity makes a pretty picture using yarn, paint, and paper.

Supplies:

tape
white bulletin board paper
yarn
ruler

scissors
red, blue, and yellow tempera paint

Setup:

Tape a piece of bulletin board paper to a table. Cut yarn into eight-inch lengths to make a large supply.

Steps:

1. Dip a piece of yarn in one color of paint.
2. Dip the same piece of yarn in another color of paint.
3. Repeatedly drag the yarn across the paper to mix the colors.
4. Repeat Steps 1–3 with another piece of yarn and a different combination of paint colors.

Annie Castillo—Education Coordinator, Dover Migrant Head Start, Dover, FL

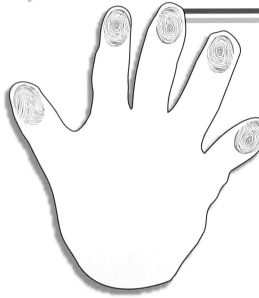

Unique Fingerprints

This one-of-a-kind fingerprint project lends itself to some science exploration! After students have finished printing, have each child use a hand lens to take an up-close look at the differences in the fingerprints.

Supplies:

4" x 6" white construction paper
pencil
washable ink pad
scissors

Steps:

1. Place your hand on the paper.
2. Trace around your hand.
3. Press a finger on the ink pad.
4. Make a print on the corresponding finger of the hand outline.
5. Repeat Steps 3 and 4 for each of the other fingers.
6. Cut out the hand outline.

Jill Davis—Grs. K–1 Multiage, Kendall-Whittier Elementary, Tulsa, OK

Lots of Dots

Build colorful pictures with this painting technique that uses blocks.

Supplies:

various colors of tempera paint
DUPLO blocks
9" x 12" white construction paper

Steps:

1. Dip a block in paint.
2. Press the block on white paper to make multiple dots.
3. Repeat Steps 1 and 2 several times using different blocks and paint colors.

Jill Davis—Grs. K–1 Multiage

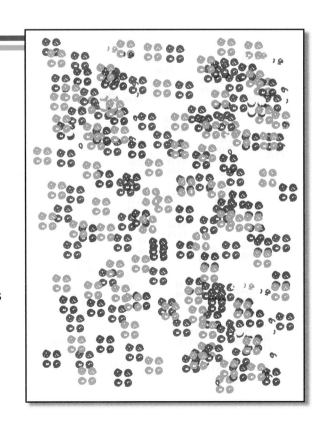

The Best Birthday Cake

A display of these personalized cakes makes a unique birthday chart. Happy birthday to you!

Supplies:

nonmenthol shaving cream
white glue
large bowl
mixing spoon
food coloring
small bowls
spoons
6" x 9" tagboard rectangle
3" lengths of pipe cleaner (candles)
yarn (frosting trim)
colored sugar sprinkles
permanent marker

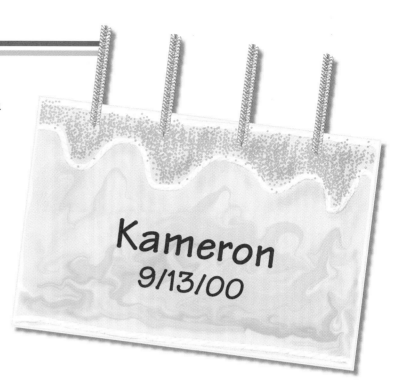

Setup:

Mix equal parts shaving cream and white glue in the large bowl to make whipped-cream paint. Divide the mixture among small bowls and tint each with a different color of food coloring to resemble frosting.

Steps:

1. Spoon a dollop of frosting onto the rectangle. Spread it with your fingers.
2. Press candles into the frosting.
3. Add trim and sprinkles. Let it dry overnight. *(Program the cake with the child's name and birthday.)*

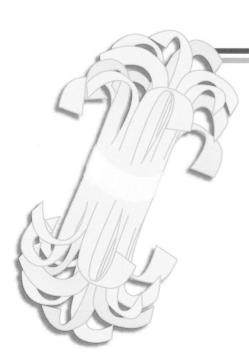

Pretty Pom-Poms

Hip, hip, hooray for some cheerful pom-poms that are sure to keep your youngsters inspired!

Supplies:

8½" x 14" colorful copy paper   scissors
tape   unsharpened pencil

Steps:

1. Beginning at a short end, roll the paper into a tube.
2. Wrap tape around the center to make a handle.
3. Fringe-cut each end of the tube down to the tape.
4. Roll each resulting strip around the pencil to curl it. Fluff the curls.

Nancy M. Lotzer—Preschool, The Hillcrest Academy, Dallas, TX

Patrol Car

Looking for a "wheel-y" cool addition to your community helpers study? This simple police car is just the ticket!

Supplies:

half a paper plate (car)
adhesive mailing label (windows)
small red paper rectangle (light)
scissors
blue tempera paint
paintbrush

2 black construction
  paper circles (wheels)
glue
large star sticker
red glitter

Setup:

Cut two notches from the paper plate so it resembles a car. Cut the mailing label in half to make two windows. Trim two corners from the red rectangle.

Steps:

1. Paint the car blue. Set it aside to dry.
2. Glue on the wheels.
3. Add the star and windows.
4. Glue on the light. Spread glue on the light. Add glitter. Allow time for the glue to dry.

Tracey Taylor—PreK Special Education, Honey Creek Elementary, Conyers, GA

Texture Alphabet

This touchy-feely alphabet display will make a lasting impression on your little learners.

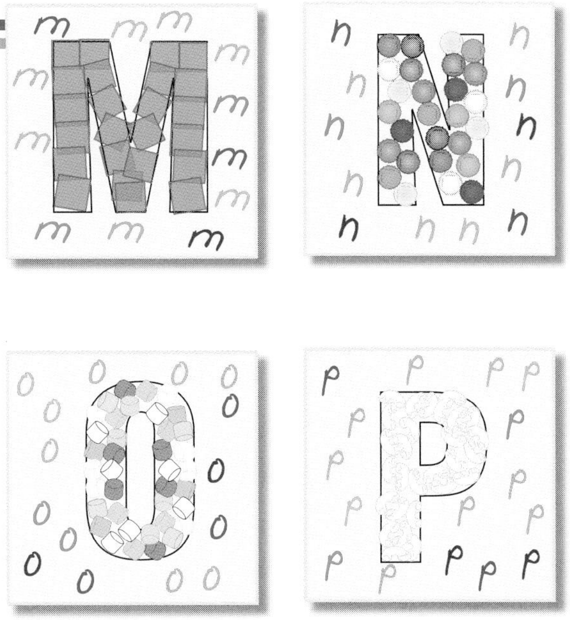

Supplies:

26 tagboard squares
assorted craft supplies
fabric and trim scraps
craft glue
markers

Setup:

Program each tagboard square with a different capital letter.

Steps:

1. Choose a letter and a type of craft supply.
2. Using different colors of markers, repeatedly write the lowercase letter around the capital letter.
3. Glue craft supplies to the letter outline. Let the glue dry.

Stacy Wingen—Gr. K, Howard Elementary, Howard, SD

Scrumptious Pie

Pies are always a welcome gift, and this cute little keeper smells just like the real thing!

Supplies:

5" aluminum tart pan
half sheet of newspaper
ground cinnamon
6" circle of tan felt (crust)
brown marker
craft glue
apple-cinnamon potpourri oil

Steps:

1. Crumple the newspaper and put it in the pan. Sprinkle it with cinnamon.
2. Draw lines around the edge of the crust to resemble a real pie's crust. Add other details as desired.
3. Spread glue around the pan's rim. Put the crust on the pie. Let the glue dry.
4. Put a drop of oil on the pie.

Cindy S. Barber—Art, Saints Cecilia and James Catholic School, Thiensville, WI

Fruity Paintings

Perk up watercolor painting with these deliciously scented paints.

Supplies:

assorted flavors of powdered
  drink mix
disposable cups
water

½-cup measuring cup
spoon
paintbrushes
construction paper

Setup:

Pour each packet of drink mix into a different cup. Add one half-cup of water to each and mix well. Put a paintbrush into each cup.

Step:

Paint a picture. Enjoy the fruity smells. Let the paint dry.

Jill Davis—Grs. K–1 Multiage, Kendall-Whittier Elementary, Tulsa, OK

Foil Painting

Try these simple yet impressive paintings when you want a project that truly shines!

Supplies:

8" square of aluminum foil
black permanent marker
watercolor paints

paintbrush
black construction paper
glue

Steps:

1. Draw a simple picture on the foil.
2. Paint the picture. Let the paint dry.
3. Mount the painting on the black paper.

Nancy M. Lotzer—Preschool, The Hillcrest Academy, Dallas, TX

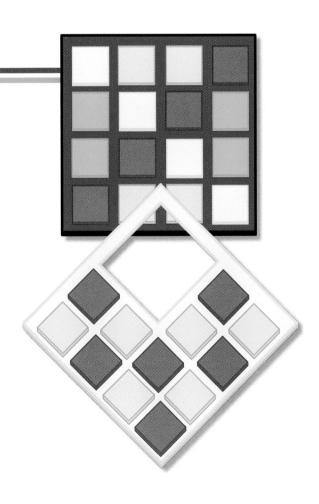

Marvelous Mock Mosaics

Make a mock mosaic into a coaster, bookmark, doorknob hanger, or anything you like. It all depends on the backing shape!

Supplies:

craft foam in a desired shape
1" squares of adhesive-backed craft foam in a variety of
colors

Steps:

1. Arrange the squares on the craft foam.
2. Peel off the backing and press each square in place.

Nancy M. Lotzer—Preschool

Special Message Easel

An old-fashioned easel bearing a special message is a welcome gift any time of the year.

Supplies:

5 craft sticks
craft glue
black construction paper rectangle
white colored pencil
small stickers (optional)
2 wooden clothespins

Steps:

1. Glue four craft sticks together to make a frame.
2. Glue the edge of the remaining craft stick to the frame to resemble a chalk tray. Let the glue dry.
3. Write a message on the black paper. Add stickers if desired.
4. Glue the black paper to the back of the frame.
5. Glue the clothespins to the frame's sides to make it stand. Let the glue dry.

Stacy Wingen—Gr. K, Howard Elementary, Howard, SD

Colorful Kings and Queens

Learning color names is an important achievement worthy of a fancy crown.

Supplies:

red, orange, yellow, blue, green, purple, and black
  3" x 6" construction paper rectangles
scissors
black crayon
small stickers in the colors listed above
3" x 18" strip of brown construction paper (headband)
glue
tape

Steps:

1. Trim one end of each rectangle to resemble a crayon.
2. Draw wiggly lines near the top and bottom of each crayon. Add stickers in matching colors to decorate each crayon.
3. Glue each crayon to the headband. Let the glue dry. *(Tape the headband to fit.)*

Cindy S. Barber—Art, Saints Cecilia and James Catholic School, Thiensville, WI

All Aflutter for Butterflies

This special technique gives white drawing paper a translucent quality. Suspend these projects in your classroom window for a high-flying display!

Supplies:

butterfly pattern on white paper
crayons
newspaper
baby oil
rag

Steps:

1. Use crayons to color in the butterfly.
2. Place the creation upside down on newspaper. Use a rag to gently rub baby oil over the paper. Allow time for the paper to dry.

Mary Lou Rodriguez—Gr. K, Primary Plus Elementary School, San Jose, CA

Spinning a Yarn

A little imagination goes a long way when little ones dip, squeeze, and cover yarn!

Supplies:

18" length of black yarn   12" x 12" waxed paper
glue in a small bowl   assorted tissue paper

Steps:

1. Dip a piece of yarn in the glue until the yarn is completely covered. Pull the yarn between two fingers to squeeze off excess glue.
2. Place the yarn on the waxed paper to create the outline of an animal shape, making sure the ends of the yarn overlap.
3. Cover the shape with tissue paper, gently pressing it onto the yarn. Allow the design to dry until the yarn is stiff.
4. Carefully remove the project from the waxed paper. *(If the sculpture isn't sturdy, place it back on the waxed paper and add more glue to the yarn.)*
5. Trim the extra tissue from the outside of the yarn.

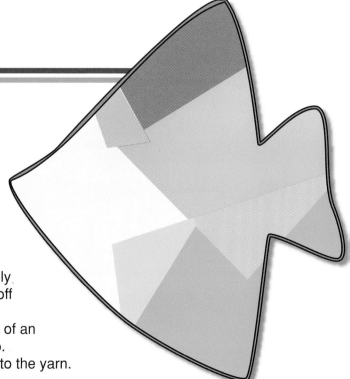

Mary Lou Rodriguez—Gr. K

Cozy Roost

Creativity finds a cozy resting place when students make these cardboard tube birdhouses.

Supplies:

4 ½" cardboard tube (birdhouse)   tape
markers   drinking straw
stickers   clay
7" construction paper half circle

Steps:

1. Use a black marker to draw a circle on the birdhouse to look like the entrance.
2. Use markers and stickers to decorate the birdhouse.
3. Form a cone from the half circle. Tape it on top of the birdhouse for a roof.
4. Tape the straw inside the birdhouse and then push it into the clay.

Deborah Garmon, Groton, CT

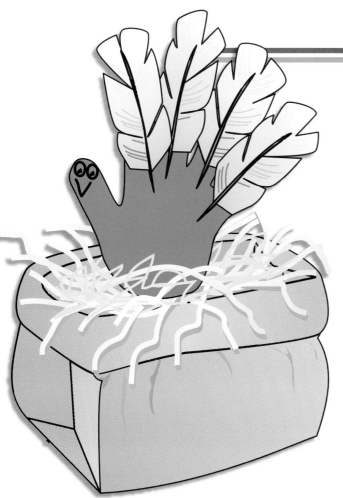

Nifty Nest

Create a nifty nest for a "hand-some" bluebird. Then display the nests on a table or counter area.

Supplies:

pencil   raffia
blue construction paper   markers
scissors   glue
brown paper lunch bag   4 blue craft feathers

Setup:

Trace a student's hand onto construction paper and cut out the handprint.

Steps:

1. Cut the bag several inches down the fold at each corner. Then fold or roll it down to make a nest.
2. Place a handful of raffia in the nest.
3. Use the markers to draw a face on the thumb.
4. Glue a feather to each finger. Tuck the bird in the nest.

Audree Barnett, Jack and Jill Early Learning Center, Norcross, GA

Pet Project

Celebrate students' favorite furry friends with this project, which is sure to wow everyone!

Supplies:

9" colored paper plate
7" colored paper plate
stapler
1" x 6" construction paper strips
scissors
assorted construction paper scraps
yarn, cut into varying lengths
glue
markers

Setup:

Staple the small plate to the large one to form an animal's body and head.

Steps:

1. Glue construction paper strips to make legs and pieces of yarn to make a tail or whiskers.
2. Use the markers and construction paper scraps to add facial features and other details.

"Dino-mite" Dinosaur

Welcome these prehistoric creatures into your classroom!

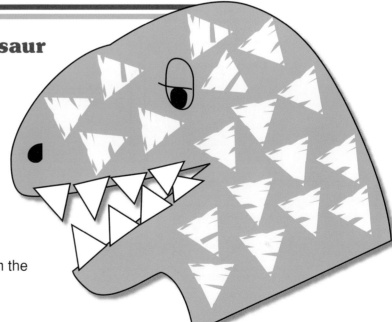

Supplies:

construction paper   shallow dish of paint
scissors   assorted shape sponges
white paper
glue
crayons

Setup:

Cut the profile of an open-mouthed dinosaur from the construction paper.

Steps:

1. Cut small triangles from the white paper and glue them in the dinosaur's mouth for teeth.
2. Use the crayons to add details.
3. Press a sponge in the paint; then press it onto the dinosaur. Repeat to make a pattern. Let the paint dry.

Debbie Clark—Preschool, Preschool in the Park, Springfield, IL

Parade of Peacocks

Paint sample strips become the colorful feathers of this friendly peacock. What a treat for the eyes!

Supplies:

seven paint sample strips   scissors
stapler   glue
blue construction paper   construction paper scraps
masking tape

Setup:

Cut out a bowling-pin shape from the blue paper for the peacock's body.

Steps:

1. Fan out the paint strips and staple them at the bottom.
2. Tape the strips onto the back of the body to serve as feathers.
3. Cut eyes, a beak, and other details from construction paper. Glue them onto the peacock.

Dawn Rolita—Gr. K, World Cup Nursery School and Kindergarten, Chappaqua, NY

Something Fishy?

Dive into this craft! You'll create a water wonderland full of cute fish and pebbles.

Supplies:

thick black marker   markers
2 sheets of clear Con-Tact paper   Fruity Pebbles or Rice
scissors   Krispies cereal
construction paper

Setup:

Draw the outline of a fishbowl on one sheet of Con-Tact paper.

Steps:

1. Cut fish shapes from construction paper. Use the markers to decorate.
2. Peel the backing off the fish bowl and place it sticky side up.
3. Press cereal pieces onto the bowl to create gravel. Then press the fish shapes onto the Con-Tact paper. *(Place the other sheet of Con-Tact paper atop the first one, sticky side down. Press the sheets together.)*
4. Trim around the fishbowl.

Robin Meinicke—PreK, Chilson Hills Head Start, Howell, MI   **149**

Funny Frog Face

It's supper time for frogs! Create a fun frog that can catch its own tasty treat.

Supplies:

pencil
white paper plate
2 sheets of green
   construction paper
scissors

glue
white construction paper
2 black pom-poms
pink or red blowout party toy

Steps:

1. Trace the paper plate onto one piece of green construction paper. Cut out the circle.
2. Glue the circle onto the paper plate.
3. Cut two green circles (eyes) from the construction paper. Glue them onto the paper plate.
4. Cut two smaller white circles (whites of the eyes) from the construction paper. Glue them onto the green circles.
5. Glue one pom-pom into the center of each eye. *(Cut a 1" x 1" X shape in the plate where the frog's mouth would be.)*
6. Push the blower toy through to serve as the frog's tongue.
7. Hold up the frog face and blow through the toy.

Lenny D. Grozier, Binghamton, NY

Barnyard Buddies

These cute critters are easy to make! Providing an assortment of fabric scraps will give students choices about whether they want to make a lamb, a cow, a pig, or another barnyard favorite!

Supplies:

2 spring-type clothespins
tongue depressor
assorted paints
paintbrushes
black fine-tip marker
assorted solid-color scraps of fabric or fleece
glue

Steps:

1. Paint the clothespins and tongue depressor the same color. Allow the paint to dry.
2. Wrap fabric around the tongue depressor to create the animal's body and glue in place.
3. Use a marker to add a face to one end of the tongue depressor.
4. Clip the clothespins onto the tongue depressor to make the animal's front and back legs.

Best Vest

Don your best vest to introduce this creative craft! After showing students some neat features—unique pockets, shaped buttons, or decorative patches—challenge each child to create his best vest design. Display a class set with the title "Our 'Vest' Efforts."

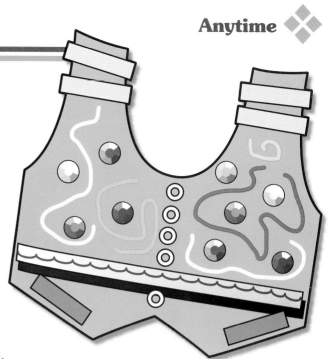

Supplies:

construction paper vest
assorted craft supplies
paper scraps
glue
markers

Steps:

1. Glue the craft supplies and paper to the vest as desired.
2. Draw to add desired details.

Gail Marsh—Preschool and Pre-Kindergarten, St. Mark's Lutheran, Eureka, MO

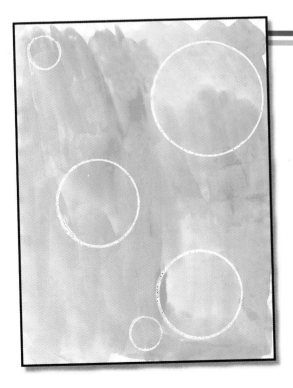

Secret Circles

Where are the secret circles? They're hidden in this mysterious painting! Not only is it fun to discover them, but it's also fun to compare paintings in the end! During a future painting session, change the shape for more fun discoveries!

Supplies:

white construction paper
white crayon
varying sizes of circle templates

dark-colored watercolor
paint
paintbrush

Setup:

Draw several crayon circles on the paper. Vary the sizes and placement on each paper you prepare.

Step:

Paint the paper to reveal the circles. Allow the painting to dry.

Gail Marsh—Preschool and Pre-Kindergarten

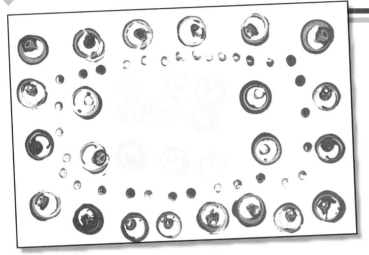

Baby Bottle Painting

Baby bottles make easy painting tools for little hands, and the end result is unique!

Supplies:

12" x 18" construction paper
shallow dishes of tempera paint
baby bottles (with nipples attached)

Setup:

Place one bottle near each different dish of paint.

Steps:

1. Dip a bottle (nipple end) into a dish of paint.
2. Press the nipple onto the paper.
   (Depending on how hard you press, you can vary the design that results.)

Lisa Toler—Preschool, Stillwater Academy, Logansport, IN

Tasty Shapes

Reinforce shape recognition and reenergize your art lesson by replacing shape templates with a variety of snacks. Be sure to reserve a few extra snacks just for eating!

Supplies:

round, square, rectangular, and triangular shaped
dry snacks (cookies, crackers, etc.)
drawing paper
crayons

Setup:

Check for food allergies before introducing the snacks.

Steps:

1. Select a snack and use it as a template to trace a shape on the paper. Continue in this manner with additional snack items until an object or scene is made. Shake off any remaining crumbs.
2. Color the picture.

Lisa Toler—Preschool

Flower Stamps

Introduce unlikely items as painting tools, and the results are simply spectacular. Artificial flowers are the focus of this activity, but why stop there? Many common household items make unique prints—just add paint!

Supplies:

artificial flowers
shallow dishes of tempera paints
construction paper
markers

Setup:

Pair each dish of paint with a different flower.

Steps:

1. Dip the head of a flower in the paint and press it onto the paper.
2. Continue with a variety of flowers and colors. Allow time for the paint to dry.
3. Use markers to add details to the painting.

Lisa Toler—Preschool, Stillwater Academy, Logansport, IN

CD Sculpture

An old CD provides a reflective platform for this free-form sculpture.

Supplies:

2" ball of modeling clay
assorted craft and household supplies
   (cotton swabs, drinking straw pieces,
   twist-ties, pipe cleaners, etc.)

old CD
hot glue gun (for
   teacher use)

Steps:

1. Work the clay to soften it; then roll it into a ball and place it on a flat surface.
2. Press assorted objects into the clay to form a sculpture. Allow the clay to dry. *(Hot-glue the sculpture to the reflective side of the CD. Let the glue harden and cool.)*

Nancy M. Lotzer—Preschool, The Hillcrest Academy, Dallas, TX

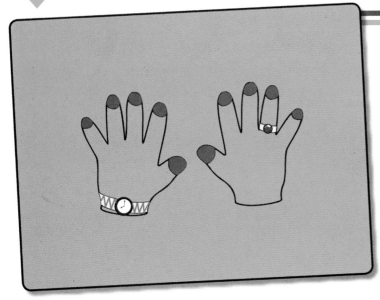

Handy Workmat

This handy mat has many uses, and the personalized design is extra special!

Supplies:

9" x 12" construction paper
fine-tip markers
crayons
craft supplies
glue

Setup:

Trace a child's hands onto the paper.

Step:

Use markers, crayons, and craft supplies to add details to the hand outlines. *(Laminate.)*

Deborah Garmon, Groton, CT

Color and Shape Collage

One color and one shape make this collage take on a one-of-a-kind look!

Supplies:

variety of materials in a single color
(wallpaper, craft foam, fabric, plastic, etc.)
scissors
9" x 12" construction paper
glue

Setup:

Select a single shape to feature, such as a rectangle. Cut the materials into the featured shape in a variety of sizes so that several will fit on the construction paper.

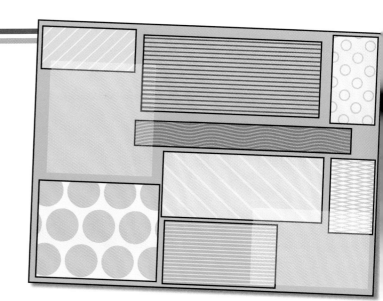

Step:

Glue the shapes on the paper in an overlapping pattern. Allow the glue to dry.

Katherine Rickin—Preschool, Mather Child Care, Cleveland, OH

Gift-Worthy Paper Magnet

The modeling mixture that is the basis for this project is easily made, easily formed, and just plain versatile.

Supplies:

1 tbsp. water
1 tbsp. glue
dish
spoon
9" x 12" colorful construction paper
medium-size hollow cookie cutter
waxed paper
glitter (optional)
2" adhesive magnetic strip

Steps:

1. Stir the water and glue together in the dish.
2. Tear the paper into one-inch pieces and stir them into the mixture. Mix well, letting the paper get thoroughly soaked.
3. Place the cookie cutter on waxed paper.
4. Fill the cookie cutter with the mixture and smooth it with your fingers.
5. Add a sprinkle of glitter if desired.
6. Remove the cookie cutter and let the mixture dry completely.
7. Attach the magnetic strip to the back.

Nancy M. Lotzer—Preschool, The Hillcrest Academy, Dallas, TX

Recipes

Use one or more of the following recipes to extend your students' art experiences. Each of these can lend itself to a variety of creative art projects and processes. So go ahead—mix it up!

Gelatin Paint

This unusual paint gives an interesting textured look to student projects.

Ingredients:
¼ c. water
¾ c. glue
any flavor gelatin

Combine the water and glue in a bowl. Add enough gelatin to achieve the desired color. Use a paintbrush to apply this paint to paper. Drying requires one or two days.

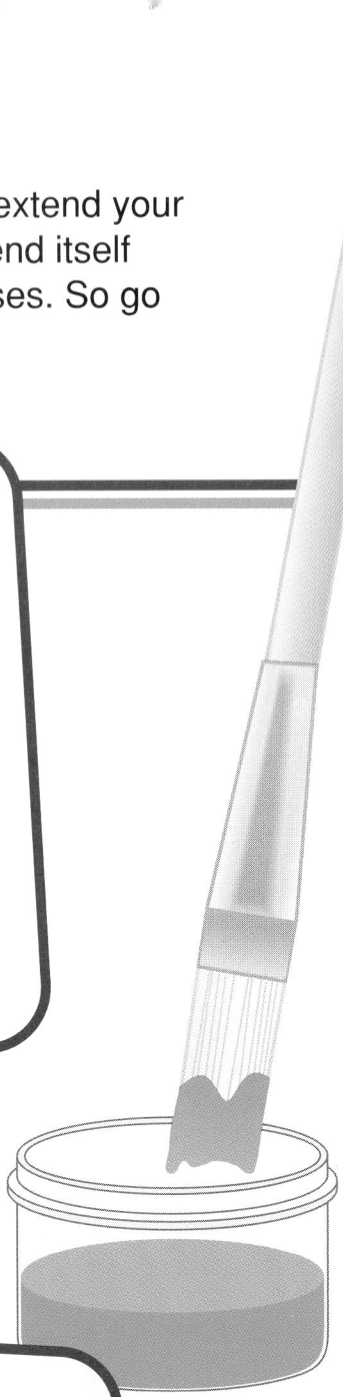

Flavored Drink Mix Paint

This paint is not only effective, but it smells great too! The scent will linger long after it's dry, so it's especially fun for painting flowers or fruit.

Ingredients:
packet of flavored drink mix
water

Dissolve a small amount of drink mix in the water. Continue adding drink mix gradually to achieve a desired color. Use different drink mix flavors to achieve an assortment of colors. Then use the paint as you would watercolors.

Milk Paint

Try using this creamy paint for a smooth pastel look!

Ingredients:
evaporated milk
food coloring

Combine evaporated milk with enough food coloring to achieve a desired color. Repeat for other colors. Try this paint on construction paper first; then experiment with other surfaces.

Cornstarch Clay

Here's an inexpensive alternative to self-hardening modeling clay.

Ingredients:
1 c. cornstarch	1 c. + 1 tbsp. water
2 c. baking soda	powdered tempera paint (optional)

Combine the ingredients in a saucepan and cook over medium heat until thick. Remove from heat and cool. Then knead well. The clay can be painted after it hardens, or add powdered paint for a desired color before the mixture cools.

Salt Dough

Mix up this no-cook version of homemade modeling dough.

Ingredients:
2 c. flour
1 c. salt
1 c. water

Mix the flour and salt together in a bowl. Slowly mix in the water. Knead the dough until it is no longer sticky. The dough can be kept in a plastic bag. If you want it to harden, air-dry it in a warm place for two to three days. Or bake it at 300° for about one hour.

My Masterpiece

Title of Artwork _____

Artist _____

Date _____

I made this using _____.

It looks like _____.

When I was working on it, I felt _____.

It's my favorite because _____

_____.

WOW!

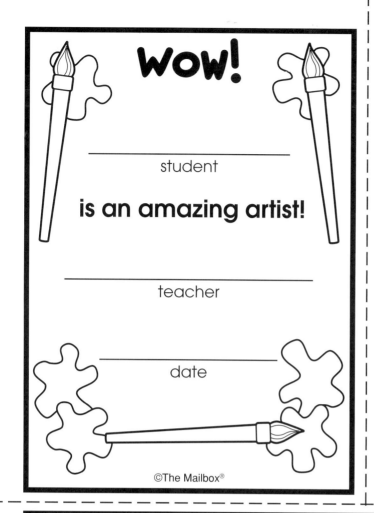

_____
student

is an amazing artist!

_____
teacher

_____
date

Look what I Made!

It's a _____.

Let's talk about it!

Love, _____
student

Check Out This Artwork!

_____
student

made _____
title of artwork

on _____.
date

Here's what you should know about this artwork:

_____

Art Supplies Request

Dear Parent or Guardian,

Our class will be making lots of fun arts-and-crafts projects. If possible, please help us by sending in the following supplies.

Sincerely,

_____
teacher

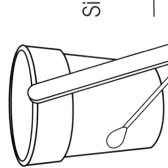

Art Supplies Request

Dear Parent or Guardian,

Our class will be making lots of fun arts-and-crafts projects. If possible, please help us by sending in the following supplies.

Sincerely,

_____
teacher